DEDICATION

Dedicated to all those who are always on the hunt for new and innovative investment opportunities and are not afraid to gain experience on their own with alternative investments.

CONTENT

Invest in P2P Lending

What you should know, how to avoid mistakes
and invest successfully

Kolja Barghoorn
Lars Wrobbel

1. Edition | October 2019

Publishing & Layout: Lars Wrobbel
Cover Design: Freshdesign.de – Ferdinand Bönisch
Proofreading: Goktug Cagri Alper, Carmen Corral
Translation: Reyyan Adels & Lars Wrobbel

ISBN: 9781693964664

Questions and Suggestions to:
lars@passives-einkommen-mit-p2p.de
kolja@aktienmitkopf.de

INTRODUCTION KOLJA BARGHOORN

Sooner or later, every person learns that it is better to build up assets instead of making debts.

Some are fortunate enough to get this somewhat trivial wisdom "cradled" by their parents in the form of a disciplined approach to money. Others, however, (including me) had to teach themselves how to handle money.

While I was over-indebted for a long time, I became more and more worried and at some point, I spent 12 to 16 hours a day working on money. This fact almost cost me my mind. I lacked money everywhere: For the rent, for the insurance and I could not even think about leisure activities. There was a shortage in every area of my life. In between, I had some cramps in my stomach when I walked to the mailbox and could see through the small window, how the bills and reminders stacked.

Luckily I have achieved a "turnaround" through discipline and a lot of work, and I'm finally free of debt. In the meantime, I even earn money on debts and have also (after a student loan for my education) changed my opinion on debts, but more on that later. Basically, there is a big difference between wealth and debt. If you take it exactly there are three big differences:

1. The assets grow in value over time. Debts also grow over time, but unfortunately not in value. The mountain of debt just gets bigger.

2. Assets bring in returns that I can spend on rent, cinema or girlfriend. Debts, on the other hand, consume income, that means no cinema and often no girlfriend.

3. Debts are not fundamentally bad, it always depends on whether you can afford it and what you use the money for.

In this book, we'd like to introduce you a way to build assets on your own, with a (still) alternative asset class. Specifically, by investing in other people's loans and thus benefiting from the ongoing interest income. Just like a bank.

Kolja Barghoorn
Magaluf – Mallorca in October 2018

INTRODUCTION LARS WROBBEL

Since I started investing in personal loans on the internet in 2014, I had to answer many questions myself in order to successfully build a stable portfolio. How does the concept really work? Which provider is the best? How do I safely build my portfolio and what does the whole thing actually look like for tax purposes? These are just a few of the issues that are important to me as a private investor on these platforms, and that you will inevitably have to face as well if you want to invest safely and successfully on P2P platforms without having a negative expectation for a long time.

In the meantime, you are holding the fourth edition of our guidebook in your hands, which has since become the standard work in the German-speaking area on P2P loans. It first appeared in 2015 and over time it has been updated many times. This is necessary because things are changing rapidly in the P2P market and we, too, are learning more and more with time. Initially, we only operated on two platforms, meanwhile, our portfolio of providers has gone more than double. I myself am now active on 13 platforms, some of which we also present here in the book. Even more has happened since the first edition. In recent years, this book has formed a P2P community on Facebook, which is now hosting over 3,000 active investors. And the associated blog www.passives-einkommen-mit-p2p.de is now one of the largest and most popular in Germany. I'm very proud that our words are so well received by you and the success stories that have come our way since then do the rest.

In February 2018, the highlight of our investment experience happened. We flew to the Baltics to see how the platforms work and to show investors here in Germany that there is more to it than a simple Ponzi scheme. We stood in real estate, which we co-financed, had meetings in offices where hundreds of people work.

We went to eat with the CEOs of each platform. An investment in P2P loans is an adventure, of course. But it has become a serious asset over the last few years, and in my opinion, it should not be missing in any portfolio these days.

Kolja and I want to use this guide to teach you the basics of P2P, give tips on how to succeed, and show you how to avoid the biggest mistakes so that you can save the money that is undoubtedly bitterly paid by beginners in the field of privately financed loans on the Internet.

As a famous saying that I like goes: "A penny saved, is a penny earned". That's why good information products in any investment field and beyond are worth gold. Few teach the sometimes hard-learned knowledge to help many build faster, more efficiently, and more cost-effectively. Concepts and ideas that have become marketable and can be used by anyone will become more transparent, understandable and easier to use in this way. Each of us, especially when it comes to finances, should feel secure in what we do and understand the products we use.

"There are thousands of ways to spend your money, but only two to earn it: Either we work for money or the money works for us."
- Bernhard Baruch -

In this sense, I wish you a lot of fun reading our guidebook. Use the information in it to save time and money, to become more successful and to avoid mistakes.

Lars Wrobbel
Delbrück – Germany in October 2018

1. P2P LOANS IN A PERIOD OF LOW INTEREST RATES

written by Henning Lindhoff, author of numerous books

The US mortgage bubble. The collapse of Lehman Brothers. The sovereign debt crisis. The rescue packages... Since 2007, a global financial and debt crisis continues, which has already massively damaged the confidence of investors and savers in the banks. And not without reason.

Since the fall of 2008, interest rates have been plummeting worldwide. For example, the yield on 10-year US government bonds is currently 1.47%.[1] The rate for German government bonds is as low as minus 0.09% that for Japanese government bonds at minus 0.3%.

This enormous fall in interest rates is the reason for all kinds of nightmares of savers. The retirement provision of experienced private investors is just as endangered as many material dreams of younger investors. And companies are also heavily burdened by the low interest rates. For example, the present value of their pension provisions is rising dramatically and reducing their equity.

Quite a few economists and almost all representatives of central banks around the world are trying to justify the decline of the interest rate culture with a milk girl's bill: They claim that there is currently a "savings surplus" that depresses interest rates. The increase in savings and the simultaneous slump in investment demand have even ensured that the natural interest rate is now in the dark.

How should one evaluate such an argument? First of all, it is important to clearly define the terms and to recognize their meaning. One must distinguish between the market interest rate and the natural interest rate. While the market interest rate is the ratio

---

[1] Effective: October 2016

between capital supply and demand for credit, the natural interest rate is an expression of human action.

Natural interest is the sum of many highly individual valuation processes, with currently available goods being valued higher than future accessible ones. The consequence is a value deduction for goods of the future.

Although the market interest rate, as the sum of natural interest, credit default premium and inflation premium, can fall to zero percent and even slide into negative territory, the natural interest rate is always positive due to the higher value of present goods.

If the natural interest was zero, this would mean that one no longer consumed anything, only saved it. He saved today, tomorrow, next week, next month, next year. He always saved. His whole life. Can you imagine that? A life without consumption?

No. And the idea of a natural interest rate of zero or less is just as absurd. But if savers and investors look for ways of asset accumulation and asset protection, they see one thing very clearly in 2018: The market interest is approaching zero threateningly. Central banks are currently managing to push interest rates far below natural interest rates. The result: Although people want to save and invest, they hardly find the opportunity.

But how do the central banks, especially the US Federal Reserve, the Japanese Nippon Ginko and the European Central Bank, manage to push market interest rates so low despite all the human favor of current capital?

For example, the European Central Bank (ECB) is buying up the government bonds of European countries to a large extent. Accordingly, the aggregate demand for government securities is, of course, higher than if only non-governmental entities, private buyers, were active in the market. The purchase prices, therefore, rise. These higher prices, in turn, lead to a decline in yields, because these are the reward for the buyer. And the more potential buyers are showing interest, the lower the issuer of the bond must set this reward.

The bond purchases of the European Central Bank ultimately lead to a minimum price policy and the establishment of a yield ceiling for government bonds. For as soon as the ECB offers for a government bond, for example, 1,000 euros, no competitor will be successful under this limit. Finally, the paper can be sold to the central bank for a guaranteed €1,000. Accordingly, the yield of this government bond will not exceed a certain percentage.

And it should not be forgotten that the ECB has set the interest rate on deposits held by commercial banks in their accounts with the central bank at minus 0.4%. Of course, the banks are trying to get away from this fine and are plunging into the low but positive government bonds. Also, returns fall and the prices of these papers rise.

So let's be clear: It is the European Central Bank and all the other central banks worldwide that have ushered in the current low interest phase and have been fueling for many months.

The question for savers and investors is now: where to go with their money? How can they still achieve a return in these times that comes reasonably close to natural interest as a reward for their consumption today?

Exactly at this point, the P2P loans come into play to enable investors to reaffirm natural interest as an expression of human action.

2. WHAT IS BEHIND P2P LOANS?

P2P is the English abbreviation for "peer to peer" and is originally from the world of computer science/informatics. It means that two computers, two so-called "peers" communicate with each other without mediation by a server. In our time of increasing digitization of all business areas, the term is also referred to as "person to person".

P2P can, therefore, mean direct communication between producer and end user, which is far better possible today than it was a few decades ago. Thanks to the Internet, more and more middlemen and intermediaries can be bypassed and thus also transaction costs in the form of money and time can be saved.

When it comes to investing, "P2P" means that a private individual conveys money to another private person or company. In the specific application of P2P loans, it is a loan without a traditional bank transaction, as we know it.

However, the concept is often not bank-free. In Germany, for example, only licensed banks can provide personal loans, and they also assume the administrative role in the background of the P2P lending business. The banks are, as required by law, the contracting parties of debtors and creditors (in Germany).

But the banks are no longer the dominant players in lending. They take a back seat, and in the foreground, peer-to-peer technology allows people, the borrowers, on the one hand, and lenders on the other, to get in direct contact again.

This book is exclusively about lending individuals to individuals or companies from an investor perspective. For P2P loans, therefore, the bank does not arrange the loan, there is a mediator between the two parties: creditors and debtors. These agents are, for example, the platforms advertised on the Internet today which include Auxmoney, Mintos, Twino, Bondora, Estateguru, and many others. Both nationally and internationally, the offer is larger and more extensive almost every day. The market has been growing rapidly for years, as shown in the following table:

Year	Volume
2005	118.000.000 $
2006	269.000.000 $
2007	647.000.000 $
2012	1.500.000.000 $
2016	18.600.000.000 $
2020 (estimated)	143.000.000.000 $

Platform Volume[2]

The Internet made it possible, and the first P2P platform was the English company Zopa, which was founded in 2005. It still exists today and at the time of writing this book with already approximately 3,000,000,000 pounds in platform volume and 360,000 members one of the largest of all European platforms.[3] Although the business area was initially restricted to the United Kingdom, since 2007, Zopa has also been expanding to Italy, the United States and Japan. In Germany, Auxmoney is currently the largest P2P platform with a loan volume of over one billion euros brokered at the time of going to press.[4]

The P2P platforms provide a type of "marketplace" where private lenders and borrowers can find each other and benefit from each other. Each vendor has its peculiarities here, as well as advantages and disadvantages (some of which we will explore more in the course of the book), but the basic principle is always based on the marketplace system offered. In doing so, the lender can choose his or her offerings on most P2P platforms, if they wish.

Each vendor also has the opportunity to incorporate a social component. For example, it only supports projects that match its preferences or personal values. This is a view that has been

---

[2] Based on data from statista.de

[3] Own Information Zopa Limited (www.zopa.com)

[4] Own Information Auxmoney GmbH (www.auxmoney.com)

completely lost in lending by a regular bank. There we have absolutely no control over our invested money and another party decides on the award.

But what is so interesting about P2P loans and why should you leave people who you do not know and whom you do not trust on a flat-rate basis, your sorely earned money? To answer this question, it makes sense to get an overview of our entire investment and to get the golden rule of capital investment on the screen, which is:

"Never put all eggs in one basket!"

Scattering your investments broadly protects you against total loss while providing quieter sleep. Later in the book, you'll learn more about this dispersion in the P2P market, which is also called diversification.

But every investor has to ask himself this question: "How wide is wide enough?" And "To what extent do my investments correlate with each other?" Nobody has any reward of it if all positions in the personal portfolio go down because of the same negative cause. Each asset class reacts differently to developments in the financial market, which is why personal loans are an interesting alternative to traditional assets such as equities, government bonds, etc. Investing more can help cushion the crashes of individual asset classes that are not that weighty anymore. We will discuss the specific correlation of asset classes with each other in a later chapter.

In addition, an investment in P2P personal loans after deduction of taxes offers a very rewarding return, behind which traditional forms of investment can sometimes be in the shade. However, it is not possible to make a definitive overall statement about the amount of the return, because this is largely dependent on each investor, mainly by the factors:

- Willingness to take risks
- Provider selection
- Loan selection
- Experience

As you can see, every investor forges his own destiny. Every passing minute, every accumulated experience, and any new information about P2P will ultimately affect your overall performance.

Of course, the social aspect for many investors can play a significant role, because you (as mentioned above) can select specific loan projects that you support or just don't support. In our current financial confusion, everyone will realize that this component is often ignored, and with the financing of personal loans, you can cover both needs: support people in their respective projects and get a good return. How many other forms of investment so obviously have this ability?

Of course, there is a moral component behind all this, which we should not disregard and which every investor should think about (some certainly more than others). For this purpose and as a suggestion, we have devoted a very own chapter to this topic, but more on that later.

We hope to have aroused your interest and that the coming pages will be a good guide for you, as a private investor, who decides to invest in personal loans, to build up appropriate knowledge to ultimately achieve a good performance in the market and to add another successful building block to your personal portfolio (however that may look like).

3. WHERE DOES P2P COME FROM AND IS IT REALLY SO NEW?

As mentioned earlier, the idea of P2P loans originated in England. After the company Zopa was launched in 2005 as the first platform on the market, followed in 2006 already with the American companies Prosper and Lending Club (the currently largest P2P platform in the world) further marketplaces. Meanwhile, the P2P idea is already slowly growing out of its infancy and established in many countries such as China, Sweden and even Saudi Arabia etc. In China, for example, there is now a huge market for P2P exchanges and now the number of P2P platforms is more than 3,000. At this time China is fighting hard to regulate the platforms.[5] Below you can see a table of 10 used and sometimes largest P2P platforms at the editorial deadline of this book:

Marketplace	Volume (08/2018)
Swaper (LVA)	42.709.010 EUR
Bondora (EST)	142.144.606 EUR
Estateguru (EST)	69.229.653 EUR
Viventor (LVA)	49.833.159 EUR
Robocash (LVA)	4.114.876 EUR
Auxmoney (DEU)	1.000.000.000 EUR
Grupeer (EST)	7.602.417 EUR
Lenndy (LVA)	13.496.068 EUR
Mintos (LVA)	978 694 482 EUR
Twino (LVA)	336.262.275 EUR

European P2P-Platforms[6]

The idea is imaginative, but not new at all, and of course, it's basically nothing world-moving, to lend a friend or a business partner a bit of money to help. Some sources date from the origins of social lending,

---

[5] More information: http://goo.gl/X9o7QK
[6] Source: Own Investigation (Effective: August 2018)

aka P2P, to the year 300 BC. Others estimate their beginnings to be around 1650 AD. Here, opinions are divided, and ultimately we will never know the exact date. Fact is, however: Since the spread of the Internet and the possibilities of Web 2.0,[7] a well-known idea in innovative form flares up again. Everyone has already lent or borrowed money, but certainly not necessarily in this way. What sets P2P apart from traditional personal loans are four key elements:

1. The purposeful loan of funds to unknown persons via a credit platform on the Internet with the aim to generate a return. This is accompanied by deliberate risk.

2. The possibility for borrowers to receive money even without a traditional loan from a bank, namely through the so-called "crowdfunding[8]". In this case, by investors who finance the loan offers. This offers not only new business opportunities for investors and companies in times of the "new economy"[9] but also alternative models to the classical bank and a chance to use the Internet with its possibilities.

3. Consideration of a loan from private individuals as an investment that can be spread across multiple loans. A loan can come from many investors and an investor can invest in many loans.

4. The central interface through a marketplace where every investor can choose which loans they want to invest in or even have the ability to automate using certain techniques.

---

[7] The term Web 2.0 refers in addition to specific technologies or innovations such as cloud computing primarily to a changed use and perception of the Internet. Users actively contribute to content and techniques, supported by innovative applications.

[8] Crowdfunding is a type of funding. Investors are a large number of people - usually consisting of Internet users, since crowdfunding is usually called up on the World Wide Web.

[9] The term "new economy" refers to the shift of the economic direction of goods production to services, in particular to web-based services.

The P2P platforms thus act as "market makers"[10] which, like stock exchanges and car dealers, ensure that supply and demand come about. Of course, the platforms want to have some of the cake for themselves, but more on that later.

So, it is not the loan as such that has been reinvented here, but it is the funding and the implementation that make up the innovative concept. As has happened so often in history, existing approaches have been improved and simplified by new ideas. And now even the banks are investing themselves in P2P companies. Morgan Stanley invests now over $100 million.[11]

---

[10] A stockbroker, which secures the market liquidity of securities and compensates for temporary imbalances between supply and demand in less liquid stocks.

[11] Article from the Financial Times of October 2013 (http://goo.gl/6ajJTf)

4. HOW DOES P2P WORK IN DETAIL?

To answer this question, we need to take a closer look at the P2P concept and try to understand the idea behind it. We all know more or less about the classic method of bank lending:

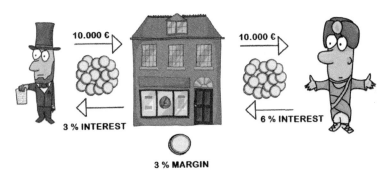

Bank lending process

On the one hand, the lenders bring their money to the bank on their savings book and receive a certain return. So in the context, they are actually savers, because they are not aware of being lenders. On the other hand, we have the borrowers who need money and get it from the bank for interest if the credit standing of the borrower allows a loan payment. The bank now pays the lender less return than it receives from the borrower. This is called "margin" and is, so to speak, the bank's profit from this simple exemplary transaction. Both borrowers and lenders have no real influence on interest rates. In this case, the bank makes all the stipulations and you cannot control the process itself. The P2P market works a little differently:

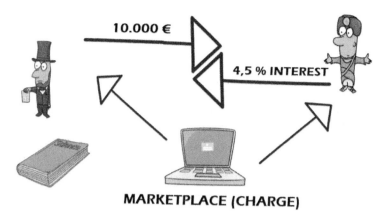

MARKETPLACE (CHARGE)

Loan procedure P2P

Here, we do have a borrower and a lender again. Unlike the bank, the lender knows consciously that he is a lender, and there are usually multiple lenders on a loan. The lender selects the borrower directly using the P2P platform, signaling investment interest. Hence the name P2P or, as already mentioned, "Person to person". The borrower pays appropriate interest here again. However, the bank is superficially lacking as an intermediary and controlling body. For the classic bank now enters a so-called P2P platform (Auxmoney, Bondora, Mintos, Twino, etc.). The sole purpose of this is to bring together both parties (borrowers and lenders) via a specially designed Internet platform. In some cases, the platform reserves some commission for this service or, just like the bank, earns margins between the borrower and lender offerings.

When investing in P2P loans, you are, therefore, consciously investing your money in credit inquiries from people you do not know. In turn, the borrower can use the money for a variety of things. For a renovation or the budding self-employment, but also for the latest flat screen or a luxury vacation. However, the borrower usually has to specify the reason for the loan first, and in some cases, you can also see him as an investor. The borrower will pay you back your money monthly after completing the loan, according to a defined repayment plan and the interest rate provided that the loan is normal and scheduled. The interest rate and repayment plan are defined by the P2P platform on the basis of influencing factors such as creditworthiness, collateral, etc. To participate in this investment, you must be at least 18 years old and register for free on one of the many P2P platforms.

Behind the P2P platforms, there are banks in Germany as well as in the rest of Europe, which ultimately pay off the funds and support the platforms. Due to legal requirements, it is even the case in Germany that lending under government decrees may only be granted by banks. P2P platforms thus only establish contact between the lender and the borrower via a marketplace on the Internet and then collect the money. If a loan is financed, the money goes to the bank and this pays out the loan to the borrower. Loan offers that have not been funded after a certain period of time will be withdrawn on many platforms. Outside Germany, however, the loans are already pre-financed, so you are **directly** invested without waiting (for example, at Mintos).

5. HOW TO INVEST AND WHO LENDS THE MONEY FOR WHAT?

You now know how the P2P concept works in theory, where it comes from and who ultimately gives the money. But now it's starting to get exciting and you'll learn how to invest money online, who actually lends money (and for what) and where investors are most likely to hang around to get their (hopefully) positive return.

The start of your investor career in the P2P market is very simple and almost the same for all providers. You register an account in your name, provide your address, usually also a bank account and in some cases, you verify yourself with an identity card. Recently, in the course of the KYC procedure, even more documents have to be uploaded in order to be paid off later or to prevent a retention of withholding tax (for example at Viainvest and Viventor).

After that, you transfer money to the platform you have selected and can usually immediately start placing your investments. This is easily recognizable by all platforms we provide, easy to understand, but of different lengths (depending on the identification procedure). We will talk about the other peculiarities of the providers we introduce in the later chapters. Now let's take a look at the following small overview of what people actually borrow money on the internet for:

Loan purpose	Percentage share
Loan consolidation	28,0%
Renovation	24,5%
Other	21,4%
Transport	8,1%
Business	6,6%
Travel	3,4%
Real Estate	3,0%
Education	2,6%
Health	2,5%

Loan purpose[12]

But who actually borrows the money? What kind of people are they? To clarify this question in its last instance is simply not possible at this point because we cannot look into people's minds. But in the area of P2P loans, there is a stubborn belief that only people who would not get a credit from their bank because of bad financial standing, would lend money. Well, if that would be true, then all P2P platforms would be of no interest to any investor because the concept would not work that way. Creditworthiness has its purpose and if only non-creditworthy people would lend money on the Internet, no positive return for the investor would be possible, but this is demonstrably not true. However, we suggest that as a prospective investor in the P2P market, you make your own image as we did. In this way, one can often best confirm or refute any upcoming opinions.

Rather, we personally believe that more and more people are discovering the simplicity and speed of online business and the benefits of Web 2.0. Another level of online banking, if you will. If you go to a bank and want a loan, it takes much longer compared to just entering data on the Internet and clicking "Apply for Credit". If the borrower then also has an excellent credit rating, he can assume that his loan project is fully funded within seconds and this without

---

[12] The graphic is based on a statistic of the P2P platform Bondora.com and is on the editorial deadline of the current edition of this book.

consultations with banks, etc. Of course, (as described earlier) here is in principle a normal bank behind it. However, the entire application process runs through the mediation platform, not the bank. Indeed, this statement does not apply if the platform does not lend itself, but only provides the platform for external credit suppliers, as it is known, for example. As it is the case with Mintos. Furthermore, one must not forget that, for example, self-employed are not so easy to get loans from a normal bank, as they have no regular income. For these people, the P2P concept is a real alternative. We will talk about this aspect in more detail later in the book.

Before we go into the providers we use, we want to clarify the question of what you should generally pay attention to when selecting vendors or what you can pay attention to. All providers logically have a website, but each P2P platform obviously reveals more or fewer details or has one or the other advantage or disadvantage over another platform. The P2P vendors may all look similar from the outside, but the visions of the platforms are often fundamentally different. This is a lesson we learned during our visits there.

The first and most important criterion for a wise investor should generally be the security of his money. We cannot avoid informing ourselves at least a little about the company we invest in. Of course, you should not only use the company's website, but also look at other relevant platforms. These include financial news, forums, blogs, independent tests, etc. A quick Google search should provide you with lots of useful information. Write everything out, what you find and try to arrange this information meaningfully. In order to give you a rough guideline for what you need to look out for, we have given you some suitable criteria that you should definitely pay attention to in our eyes and that you should research. You can see these in the following list:

- Where is your money stored? (Which bank is behind it?)
- What is the security limit for your uninvested capital? (if there is one)
- What is the current situation of the company? (Research current news)

- Is it a new company or has it been on the market for years? (There are providers that have been on the market for a long time or providers with innovative techniques for improving returns)
- What collateral does the company offer investors? (Do borrowers possibly have to deposit property or similar assets for the possibility of a loan default?)
- How does the placement platform behave in the event of loan defaults and what does it do against it (every reputable company should have a dunning and collection procedure and make this transparent for the investor as well)
- Does the P2P platform have a credit rating system? If so, is it transparent and understandable?
- How transparent does the borrower have to be and do you get enough serious information about your credit behavior and the project to be funded?
- Does the platform have support?
- Does the P2P platform have special forums or groups to exchange investors with each other? Or are they elsewhere on the internet? (This may sometimes give you information about loan applications that you might not see from the beginning of your experience)
- What is the average interest rate level of the platform?

As always, you have to decide for yourself how many criteria you want to fulfill and what risk you are willing to take. No platform will be able to meet all criteria. The principle should always be:

"The more information is available and the more transparent and understandable they are, the better."

In the following chapters, we will look at some well-known but very different providers for some of these criteria and show you the pros and cons. So if you want to start fast and do not want to spend a lot of time researching, these chapters will be very interesting for you as you will learn about these providers everything you need to start as an investor. We are currently investing in all the vendors we have to offer, so we have the experience to give you a hopefully helpful picture. In addition, guest author Claus Lehmann will introduce you to two of his favorites. However, these chapters are not about promoting the platforms we've presented, but about concentrating all the information you need about the platforms and making them available in one place. Where you invest and if you follow our suggestions will ultimately be up to you.

Of course, the picture may change over the next few months and years, so it's important to stay alert, keep checking the market for new providers, and perhaps spend some money trying one or the other. You will always be able to gain more experience with a real investment as a test than relying on external factors and information from the internet. Tasting is about studying. This principle applies here as well. And Aristotle said:

"One has to believe the observation more than the theory and the theory only if it leads to the same result as the appearance itself."

6. TYPES OF P2P PLATFORMS
written by Carmen Corral, publisher of
Invertir en Préstamos P2P

P2P Marketplaces

A marketplace is an intermediary between investors and originators. Most of the P2P platforms are marketplaces.

The platform brings together the loans issued by several different credit originators and presents them to its investors. The borrower applies for a loan with an originator. Then the originator offers the loan to investors in the marketplace to be funded. Once the loan is funded, the originator lends the money to the borrower. The credit originator is in charge of the relation, process and operations with the borrower.

Marketplaces work with many originators and frequently with different kind of loans too. In some cases, they included not just P2P but P2B, invoice financing and real estate loans too.

For investors, marketplaces are great to diversify investments between credit originators within the same platform.

Although not all of the platforms publish who are the credit originators, most of them do, offering transparency to the investor.

These are some P2P marketplace platforms: Mintos, Peerberry, Grupeer, Fast Invest.

P2P Loans Platforms

These are companies that handle both the borrower and investor part of the operation. Returns could be higher as there is no intermediary but not always.

When you invest in these platforms you can diversify in loans, but you are investing in the same credit originator. That means you rely on the procedures and administration of a single company for all the loans you are investing in.

As you are trusting your money to the same credit originator, it is potentially riskier. Although, it is easy to reduce this risk investing in different platforms, that way you diversify between originators too.

Some P2P loan platforms in this category are Bondora, Bitbond, Zank, Neo Finance, Finbee.

Real Estate Platforms

Real Estate platforms are growing fast. They bring the opportunity for small investors to have access to the profitability of property investments. These kinds of platforms specialized in investments in real estate, including loans with property guarantee, development projects, buy to let or buy to sell properties.

Depending on the type of project you invest in you will receive interests monthly or at the end of the period. Usually, Real Estate platforms don´t have buyback guarantee, however having a property as a guarantee tend to be a good measure against the risk of default.

These are some real estate platforms: Estateguru, Reinvest24, Rendity, Bulkestate, Housers.

P2B (peer to business) Platforms

These platforms specialized in loans to companies, usually SMEs that seek financing to expand or cover the needs of their business. They could include business loans to business expansion, to launch a new product, crowdinvesting projects, etc.

Information about every loan or project is usually more detailed than in other platforms. Usually, P2B platforms have fewer projects available to invest compared to P2P platforms. The projects and loans they offer required a more thorough credit evaluation than consumers loans.

Flender, Crowdestor and Envestio are examples of P2P platforms.

7. BONDORA

Miscellaneous

Bondora is a well-known Estonian P2P platform. It was founded in 2009 and is one of the largest platforms in the Baltic States with a lending volume of more than 120 million euros.[13] Bondora is also a well-known asset to many young investors in Germany, as it offers very attractive returns and also offers credit investment to investors outside Estonia. Bondora currently offers loans in Estonia, Finland and Spain. Bondora is already a very old "hare" in the business and even expands beyond the borders of his country of origin.

It is only possible since 2012 for foreign investors like us to invest in Bondora. The Bondora website is by default in English, but you can easily switch to German. Now and then you still find the one or the other spelling mistakes, which makes the understanding a bit difficult, but generally we classify the usability as good. The website has been working on a regular basis since the start of our investments. On the one hand, it is nice that something is constantly expanding and improving, but on the other hand, it can happen that you have to look for known functions more often. However, Bondora regularly informs investors about news and improvements via a detailed investor newsletter and, more recently, with its own YouTube channel[14]. We, therefore, assume that quality will continue to improve over time.

After registering at Bondora, you must use a specified bank account to fill your virtual account with funds from abroad by bank transfer. The identification of the transfer is made possible by a personal reference, which has to be indicated during the transfer. Once the money has arrived at Bondora, it is ready for investment. The easy-to-reach return on Bondora is tremendously high and most investors, according to the company, generate on average 15 to 25% return on Bondora.

---

[13] Based on data from February 2018

[14] bit.ly/BondoraYouTube

The minimum investment is only 1 Euro, which makes it possible to diversify sensibly even with tiny investment amounts, and above all, you can start with very little money. Since there are two marketplaces at Bondora, the platform also had two different pricing models until some time ago. In the primary market, investments were generally free of charge and on the secondary market, Bondora charged a fee of 1.5%. Meanwhile, however, both the first and secondary market is free. We assume that this will remain so for now.

Safety

Behind Bondora, there is the Estonian branch of SEB Bank, one of the largest banks in Sweden, which manages the funds and calls itself AS SEB Pank[15]. It is part of the Estonian deposit insurance[16], the limit of which is currently 100,000 euros. But keep in mind that this applies maximum for uninvested funds. Bondora confirms on its own website that the accounts are paid out in the event of corporate bankruptcy.[17]

In security matters, Bondora is very restrictive, which should give the investor additional confidence in the platform. If you apply for a loan from Bondora, you have to prove the following things:[18]

- The borrower must be in paid employment and have sufficient income to fully meet the monthly expenses.
- The borrower must not have a bad credit history, such as arrears, late payments, previous bankruptcy or open enforcement.
- The borrower may not have received a payment request within the last two years.
- The borrower may not be a convicted criminal or a civil suit.

---

[15] Further information can be found at: http://www.seb.ee/eng

[16] In Estonia the security limits differ according to the type of assets to be protected. Deposits at a bank (sight, time deposits and saving deposits) have been secured from January 1st, 2011 to 100 percent to a maximum of 100,000 Euros.

[17] https://support.bondora.com/hc/en-us

[18] https://support.bondora.com/hc/en-us/articles/212798869-Borrower-application

- The borrower must have had no gambling problem in the past.

With such criteria, Bondora already absorbs much of the uncertainty for the investor and can thus ensure that there are no borrowers from the outset whose sole purpose is to collect money from good-faith investors.

Bondora also offers a credit rating system. First, external credit service providers (eg Krediidiinfo for Estonian loans) classify borrowers in degrees ranging from AA to HR, where HR stands for very insecure and AA for very secure loans. Based on the final credit rating, Bondora also determines in advance the maximum amount of the loan, its minimum interest rate and the severity of the financial analysis (receipts, account statements, etc.).

Loan default

If a borrower becomes insolvent at Bondora, a standardized dunning and collection process exists. Bondora uses a three-level and largely automated dunning and debt collection procedure. It is continued until the overdue amount is fully repaid or the receivable is written off. The goal is to prevent customers from meeting their debt obligations. In stage 1, the debtor is informed by SMS and calls about the late payment. If no success occurs here, a collection agency will take over the further work. Stage 2 is the legal action against the debtor should he not have already repaid his debt. Stage 3 deals with cases where a full repayment after stage 1 and 2 is unlikely (eg personal bankruptcies or deaths).[19]

The whole process can take years and is additionally dependent on the respective region. Each case and the amount of the repayment is, therefore, very individual to see. At the editorial deadline of this book, our quota of those loan projects that had crossed the magic "60-day-overdue-limit" was around 24%. In the section "secondary

---

[19] You can find further information on the collection process of Bondora here: https://support.bondora.com/hc/en-us/sections/203115469-Credit-and-investment-risks

market" you will find out that Bondora offers other ways to deal with overdue loans.

Communications

The support can be written in English and also several other languages. The borrowers themselves cannot be contacted directly. However, in the investment marketplace, there was the opportunity to ask general questions about the loan project, which all other investors could then see. The borrower could answer this for the general public. Unfortunately, Bondora has disabled the Demand feature, which, as we find, is a great pity as the manual investor is given a bit of transparency and potentially useful information.

Also, the forum that Bondora has offered earlier, unfortunately no longer exists today. Likewise, there are no closed investor groups to exchange. Bondora is thus moving towards an automated investor tool rather than an interactive marketplace.

Secondary market

The Bondora secondary market is a peculiarity to many other P2P platforms and you should familiarize yourself with it. It is intended to sell investments made by you or to buy investments that have been made by others. Some investors take this opportunity to quickly increase their portfolio and make "bargains" - for example, on loans that are already in a dunning stage. Partly you can buy in this way cheap investment with 20, 30 or even more percent discount. However, on the other hand, of course, you also accept an increased default risk.

Meanwhile, you can even sell loans on the secondary market, which are already over 60 days overdue and thus already in the collection process. Before that, Bondora set a strict limit at 60 days overdue. In our experience, it has proven to be a good and viable means of selling just overdue loans on the secondary market to avoid the risk of default and still get the bulk of your investment back (sometimes even more than that). However, it can also happen that nobody buys your loan. In this case, you have to set up a corresponding discount for the future investor, which logically means a loss for you.

Bondora initially charged a fee of 1.5% of the loan sales price, which has now been canceled. As a guideline for stopping a successful sale offer of an overdue investment, it should not take more than 40 days, if possible. We suggest hiring it at a discount of 20-30% between the 30th and 40th day, depending on the competitive offer at the time, and only if you want to avoid further risk with a safe loss. If you want to be serious in the secondary market, you should find here for you a system that works permanently and test a lot.

Of course, there are also investors who only use the secondary market and who have developed strategies and opportunities for doing so. In the chapter "secondary market" we asked the second market specialist and P2P expert Andreas Tielmann of p2p-anlage.de to explain to you exactly how the secondary market works to give you a better insight. Because we both honestly do not use the secondary market actively and only occasionally for testing purposes.

Our experiences with Bondora

Bondora is a great and profitable platform for any serious investor in the P2P sector, which you should not disregard. In addition to our experience as investors, we visited Bondora in Tallinn in February 2018, learned a lot about the platform and were able to gain additional insight. The Estonian P2P platform follows a proven concept for many years and is almost no longer a Fintech-startup with a business age of 10 years. The office still feels that way. Everything is colorful, the employees are in a good mood, and work-life balance is always taken care of. One would be happy to invest here.

We see a big advantage in the simplicity compared to platforms, which are to be managed with a lot of manual work. With Portfolio Builder, we spend only a fraction of the time at Bondora to make a return on investment (in our view). The Portfolio Builder at Bondora (called "portfolio manager") has very few setting options and is, therefore, easy to configure. In a previous version of the Portfolio Builder, there were no mandatory settings that had to be accepted, but you could adjust your portfolio according to your own risk profile.

Bondora Portfolio Builder (old)

Bondora Portfolio Builder details (old)

The new portfolio manager from Bondora offers, as already mentioned, far less setting options, but it is all the easier to use:

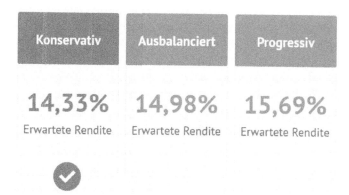

Bondora Portfolio Builder

Now, you have the option to choose from several suggested strategies, including conservative, balanced and progressive. Depending on the setting, your portfolio builder will, therefore, invest rather low-risk or high-risk, which of course, translates into your expected return, as the following graph shows:

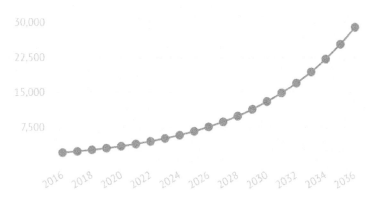

Expected return Bondora Portfolio Builder

If money is available in your virtual account, Bondora will immediately start auto-investing as soon as you choose a model and activate it. A fast, transparent and easy thing.

If you're more of a friend of Portfolio Builder's detailed configuration, you can now even connect to your account through a third-party via the Bondora API.[20] The market is still quite new and there are not too many offers yet. However, the BeePlus platform offers a quick solution.[21]

Incidentally, Bondora has also been using the Bondora Portfolio Pro since 2017. With this, it is possible for you to adjust your investment again somewhat more granular, which enormously enlarges the possibilities for you as an investor.

---

[20] https://support.bondora.com/hc/en-us/articles/213691009-What-is-the-Bondora-API-

[21] You can register for free at: https://beeplus.me/

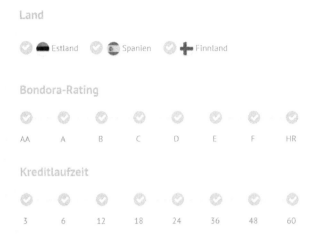

Land

Estland   Spanien   Finnland

Bondora-Rating

AA   A   B   C   D   E   F   HR

Kreditlaufzeit

3   6   12   18   24   36   48   60

Bondora Portfolio Pro

There is a so-called "queue system" at Bondora, which ensures that the use of the Portfolio Builder is fair. In principle, we are talking about an investor queue, where everyone has their turn sometime. Example: Investors A and B each set up an activated portfolio builder with the same criteria, and places 1 (Investor A) and 2 (Investor B) in the queue system. Now, if a loan of the best credit rating is set, Investor A gets the bid due to the better placement in the queue system, but then slips to second place and investor B is in the first place.

Another helpful tool is the already mentioned secondary market at Bondora. Due to the fact that it is no longer chargeable, the secondary marketplace opens up many new ways to experiment and invest at a low cost. Since the secondary market is not available at most of the other provider, this is another plus for Bondora in our eyes. Of course, this is not automatically operable, but it is up to the individual, how much effort he wants to put in the secondary market. You can either invest cheaply or sell investments to quickly get cash or even escape a threat of debt collection. In any case, as an investor, you have a bit more control over your portfolio.

But that was not all! Since mid-2018, Bondora has been using the new tool Go & Grow, which makes it extremely easy for you to enter the world of P2P loans. Bondora Go & Grow is also an automatic loan portfolio, but with daily availability. As a result, it almost feels like a bank account where you can get daily your money. The advantages at a glance:

- Immediate liquidity, you can withdraw your money at any time.
- You will receive interest only on withdrawal. This leads to a tax-efficient effect.
- It's extremely easy for beginners to finish depositing.
- Free of charge, there is only a lump sum of 1 EUR withdrawal fee.

There is a 6.75% target yield on this portfolio, which seems a little underpriced, as it is by no means guaranteed, remembering that this is risk capital as well. Bondora says Go & Grow has a diversified credit portfolio with advanced technology. This is based on their many years of experience and is intended to secure investors' portfolios in the long term. This product is great for parking short-term cash reserves, as we both did. Meanwhile, there are also many more testimonials from experienced bloggers on the net who use the system to optimize their cash position. A test of Bondora Go & Grow can be found on the blog. Please keep in mind that this technology is still in its infancy and time will tell if the concept prevails or not.

Everything you have read here, Bondora completes with a security model, which requires evidence of the borrower according to individual criteria to secure your investment. Bondora seeks to provide the investor with a great deal of transparency, which we find good and gives us an additional sense of security.

Furthermore, we were very pleased with the overview and the reporting capabilities of our own portfolio. You can draw on a myriad of ways to get detailed information about your portfolio: Upcoming monthly income, predicted income over the next months, and much more will give you a detailed overview. What seems a bit overloaded at the beginning, turns out to be a useful addition to any investor after some time and, among other things, is really fun:

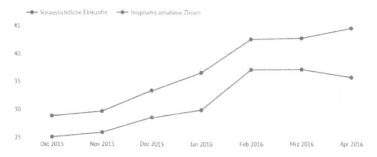

Statistics of Bondora

Nevertheless, one should not ignore the risk. For returns that are up to 50% (if you invest in appropriate rating classes or use the secondary market), you will almost certainly lose investment and you have to be aware of that. But it is up to you to use the tools provided by Bondora wisely and minimize the risk.

If something does not go the way you want, you can still try to sell an overdue investment through the secondary market. Furthermore, according to our observation, there is still much work on the Web presence of Bondora and also in the scope of functions. So what you read here could be obsolete again in a few months and have developed both positively and negatively. It is therefore: "Watch out when buying eggs!"

8. MINTOS

General

Mintos is still a very young supplier from Latvia with headquarters in the capital Riga. Founded in early 2015, investors from the European Union and also from Switzerland can invest their funds here. Borrowers can be both individuals and businesses. Meanwhile, Mintos lends credits in several different countries: among them, there are the Czech Republic, Latvia, Estonia, Lithuania, Georgia, Poland and many more in Europe. You can even invest your money in China, Africa and South America. Despite the fact that Mintos is still a relatively young company, the mediated monthly loan volume at the time of going to print of this book is already almost 50 million euros, and the trend is rising. More than half a billion loans have been lent.

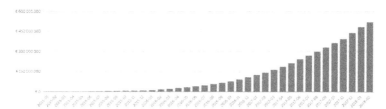

Development of Mintos

The Mintos website is very simple and easy to use. In our eyes, the Mintos team has put a lot of effort into making it easy for the investor to get on with a quick and easy overview. As with Bondora, we suspect that the website will still change occasionally because of the age of the company.

At Mintos, the registration process is just as easy as with Bondora, and here, too, the advance payment principle including the virtual account applies. The transfers go to the Nordea-Bank[22] via SEPA procedure abroad. According to Mintos, the average net yield for investors is around 12-13% at the time of going to press on this book. The type of loans include the mortgage loans, secured car loans, business loans, consumer loans (with 3/4 the largest share) and the so-called factoring together. Factoring is still relatively new. Here you invest in invoices from small to medium-sized companies to large corporations. But now there are many other types of loans online that you can easily research directly on Mintos. The loan amount is on average 8,000 euros and has terms of only a few days to several years. The highest loan amount is over 100,000 euros, the lowest at less than 100 euros. The minimum investment for investors at Mintos is 10 euros.

Mintos has 3 nice major features that we should discuss more in detail:

First, all loans are already pre-funded by Mintos. This means that the funds have already been disbursed to the borrowers, are in the repayment phase and there is no lead time for investors. So when you invest money in a loan, it is instantly created on the visible terms and no longer goes through a bidding phase.

Second, many loans at Mintos are secured by real estate. Mintos has a partner company (Latio[23]), which carries out a valuation of the real estate. The borrower may then submit a credit request up to a maximum of 90% of the valuation value. It is also nice that you can even look at the real estate objects with photos and reports.

---

[22] Excerpt from Wikipedia: Nordea (Nordic Ideas) is a leading financial group in Northern Europe and the Baltic States. The largest shareholders are the Swedish state with 13.5%, the Sampo Group with 21.4% and the Nordea Fonden with 3.9%. The bank is one of the 28 major banks classified by the Financial Stability Board (FSB) as a "systemically important financial institution". It is therefore subject to special monitoring and stricter equity requirements

[23] Further information can be found at http://latio.lv/en

Third, Mintos gives a buyback guarantee. This means that loans are automatically repurchased after 60 days of default. As a result, failures can be avoided and the return can be calculated better. However, not all loans at Mintos have a buyback guarantee. Only loans with a corresponding identification have this security. So it pays to pay attention to safety. You will learn later that the buyback guarantee is not as secure as it seems.

Incidentally, the real estate loan also generates an important Mintos ratio, the LTV (Loan-to-Value) or the lending rate. The investor can later use this for the configuration of his portfolio builder. The lower the lending rate, the safer the loan, but the lower the return. For a better understanding here the official example of Mintos: You have a loan amount of 20,000 EUR. If the loan is borrowed for EUR 12,000, this would mean an LTV of 60%, with a mortgage of EUR 20,000 an LTV of 100%. Accordingly, the first variant would be less risky.

As far as the fee structure is concerned, Mintos currently provides a sound basis for your investments. A few months after the opening of Mintos, investor fees (then 2%) were canceled for investors. Since then you have been investing free of charge on both the primary and the secondary market.

Security

According to Mintos, in an insolvency scenario, investors in the Mintos database will receive all information about all transactions conducted through the portal. A liquidator or insolvency administrator handles the transfer of all investments as well as the loan service. In order to guarantee proper implementation of this regulation, Mintos has entered into a guarantee agreement with the legal entity FORT[24] on the basis of which Mintos forwards the data of the website to a data store on a monthly basis and FORT stores this data securely.

A credit rating system like Bondora does not exist with Mintos. However, for different types of loans, there are different collateral

---

[24] Further information can be found at: http://fortlegal.com/

for the lender. So you can, for example, see a concise financial analysis of the company.

Another huge security aspect is the buyback guarantee. Car loans, for example, are almost always secured and thus you cannot lose your money (in theory).

Loan default

Mintos has a debt collection process, which is managed by the internal debt recovery team. Should a loan default, Mintos attempts to reach the defaulting debtor by e-mail, telephone or post to determine the reason for the delay. Depending on the situation, Mintos may offer to restructure the loan or take other appropriate measures designed to avoid further deterioration of the loan situation and thus protect the investor from a loss. If the borrower is in default of payments for more than 60 days and several attempts to improve the situation have been unsuccessful, Mintos may initiate a compulsory expropriation of the property or other court orders.

Communications

Mintos offers support via phone and e-mail. The email support from Mintos makes a very good and professional impression on us. Our communication was exclusively in English and all inquiries were answered within a few hours. A little tip: If you use a Google account for your emails, you will often see photos of the employees. With the beautiful staffing of Mintos, the investment is even more fun.

Furthermore, Mintos operates a website-internal blog[25] with the latest news around the P2P market, Mintos itself and many other topics. The comment function is activated, so that one can come here also in direct, topic-relevant dialogue with Mintos. Mintos does not offer a direct dialogue with the borrowers. So all you get is the information about a loan that Mintos gives you, and that's not really much, unlike Bondora. In our opinion, this is not absolutely necessary and so completely sufficient.

---

[25] You can find the blog at http://blog.mintos.com/

Secondary Market

Like Bondora, Mintos offers a secondary market where on-going or overdue loan projects can be sold to avoid collection procedures and to get your funds back sooner if necessary. In addition, this of course, offers you the opportunity to grab one or two bargains to boost your portfolio low. On the picture below you can see the main view of the secondary market, as shown on the Mintos website:

Secondary market-view Mintos

The secondary market is just as powerful an instrument here as the competition Bondora. But again, the premise is that you have to deal with it if you want to include it as a useful tool in your portfolio strategy, because an automated investment is not possible here. However, as a seasoned investor, you can achieve tremendous returns in a short amount of time that would not be possible through the normal initial market investment.

Our experiences with Mintos

In our opinion, it pays to take a closer look here, because Mintos has a great advantage over many other P2P platforms with its multitude of secured loans. At the time of writing this book, there are now many providers with a buyback guarantee.[26] After a couple of vendor presentations, you should now also slowly recognize how individual the different platforms can be and that you should not shun the P2P industry generally in general, as critics unfortunately only too often do. This was also evident during our visit to Riga. Mintos is a P2P

---

[26] For example, the platforms Mintos, Twino, Viainvest, Robocash, Viventor and many more currently offer a full buyback guarantee.

platform with a big vision, because it wants to become the largest marketplace in the world and lend in all countries of the world. What initially looked like a bad marketing gimmick, could soon become a reality, because the growth of the platform is unprecedented and jokingly we call Mintos, therefore, always the Amazon of the P2P industry.

The returns on Mintos are very tempting. But as we know, the return comes from the risk and this is mainly due to the fact that Mintos is still a very young company and you have to keep an eye on the development in order to be successful in the long run. However, this recommendation applies in general to all P2P platforms. Mintos works differently than many other providers: They merely provide a platform on which many external service providers now offer their loans. So, if you diversify properly here, Mintos is (in our eyes) a safer platform than many others.

Also with the automation Mintos can score. The Portfolio Builder (called Mintos "Auto-Invest") is easy to set up, does all the work for the investor and can be easily adjusted at any time. As a special customization option, you can even run multiple portfolio builders in parallel on different strategies. You can thus take another step in personal portfolio diversification this way. For example, you could do the following setting of Portfolio Builder:

Auto-Invest 1: 70% of your available capital is invested in a safety-oriented manner with average interest rates and a low mortgage lending value. In addition, you only invest in secured Estonian car loans.

Auto-Invest 2: 30% of your available capital is invested in return-oriented high interest rates and high lending value, including consumer credit, across all of Mintos possible countries.

You see, what offers itself here for individual possibilities? Do you want more settings? No problem for Mintos! In the picture below you can see other configurations offered by the Mintos Portfolio Builder. You can really let off steam, test and ultimately find the perfect setting for you and your portfolio. Use this possibility too.

Settings Mintos Auto-Invest

The options are very simple, yet granular enough to make important selections. As you have already seen in the introduction of multiple portfolio builders, another difference with the other providers is that you can even select different loan types here. Do you have a problem lending money to people who go on vacation with your money or buy the latest flat-screen TV? No problem, probably the fewest investors like it. At Mintos, in this case, you simply take out the consumer credit from your portfolio management and the job is done.

Similar to Bondora, we like the secondary market on Mintos very well. It's great to have the opportunity to get your money quickly and beat the bargain, on the other hand. If you do it right, you can give your portfolio a few percentage points of additional return.

All in all, this very young provider makes a great impression on us and we are curious to see where the road goes and whether Mintos can continue the trend that has been set. At the editorial deadline of this book, Mintos has already surpassed Bondora light-years in terms of lending volume.

If you want to see some examples of Mintos practice or if you would like to know exactly how the Portfolio Builder is configured correctly, check out the Lars blog.[27] Since Mintos is currently the most popular P2P platform, you will find a whole series of interesting articles there that will provide you with free added value and hopefully take your investment to a new level.

---

[27] https://passives-einkommen-mit-p2p.de/category/mintos/

9. TWINO

General

Founded in early 2015, Twino is, like Mintos, one of the most popular P2P consumer credit platforms in Europe. The Twino platform is headquartered in the Latvian capital Riga and sells loans from European countries Georgia, Latvia, Poland, Denmark, Russia, Spain and Kazakhstan. At Twino, only consumer loans up to EUR 3,000 are currently being brokered. In terms of lending volume, Twino has even surpassed the much more experienced and older Bondora platform with its strong start. And the trend continues to show strong upward, as the following diagram illustrates very nicely:

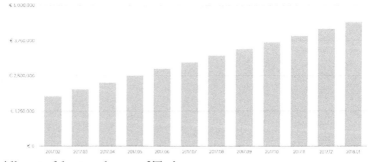

Allocated loan volume of Twino

Twino, like Mintos and Bondora, also works with a large bank. In this case, Swedbank[28] is one of the largest banks in Northern Europe. Investors from all over Europe have the opportunity to invest in the marketplace after registering. The minimum amount for a primary market investment is currently 10 euros. According to the

---

[28] Further information about Swedbank:
https://en.wikipedia.org/wiki/Swedbank

platform itself, the average return on investment is between 10% and 12%.[29]

At the present time, the platform is completely free on both the primary and secondary market. Like many other platforms, Twino finances the lending business with spreads between lending rates offered to lenders and borrowers.[30]

At Twino, you mainly invest in so-called payday loans[31], which are quite popular. The advantage of these payday loans lies in their extremely short terms of often only one month. For investors who only want to park their money for a very short time, this is a great advantage.

The website of Twino is very easy to use. There are not too many configuration options, the market place is quite simple and tidy. The user interface is now available in many languages. The registration is just as easy as with the other platforms. You create your account, verify yourself via your ID card, and transfer some money, which is within 3 days (usually faster) on Twino and then you can start.

Security

Twino used to be known as Finabay[32], a platform that lends across Europe. Twino has successfully brokered over €250 million in lending since 2009 and has been known in the industry for years for developing innovative financial services. All loans that can be found on the marketplace are, therefore, also serviced by Twino as a loan partner.

---

[29] Current statistics are available here for retrieval: https://www.twino.eu/en/profile/investor/statistics

[30] A comprehensive FAQ on all current questions can be found at: https://www.twino.eu/en/profile/investor/how-it-works/investing

[31] Further information on short term loans: https://en.wikipedia.org/wiki/Payday_loan

[32] You can find further information about the Twino foundation by Finabay here: https://www.twino.eu/en/profile/investor/about/quick-facts

For this reason, the platform can also serve a more and more popular tool: the buyback guarantee. It states that any loan that is overdue for more than 30 days will be repurchased by Twino and thus (theoretically) have a fail-safe portfolio on Twino. But you should always be aware that the buyback guarantee merely shifts the risk and does not completely offset it. If, for example, Twino can no longer service the buyback guarantee, it is questionable what will happen. Until recently, all loans at Twino were covered by the buyback guarantee. So you did not even have the opportunity to stumble into a consumer loan that will not be repaid, something that can happen to you at Mintos, for example. Meanwhile, however, loans are offered without a repurchase guarantee. You can select the loans specifically or have them selected through the Portfolio Builder to invest only in secured loans.

Loan default

A loan default can (in theory) as we said, for most loans never happen. At least you as an investor cannot care less about the buyback guarantee. Thus, there is no official collection process for you that can be checked and that you can track. The collection process is outside the borrower/lender relationship on the platform and is the sole responsibility of Twino.

However, the borrower has the option to extend the loan for a fee. This so-called "extension" allows the borrower further leeway in the repayment of his installments. For you as an investor, this is not a problem, but rather an advantage! During the extension, Twino pays you the interest. The maximum extension is one month and can be requested up to 6 times. Twino will automatically buy back your share for the seventh time.[33]

---

[33] You will find everything worth knowing on this topic also in the Twino FAQ:https://www.twino.eu/en/profile/investor/how-it-works/investing

Communications

You can reach the support of Twino in several ways: via e-mail, telephone and even "fintech-like" and comfortably via the Skype chat during normal business hours (no 24-hour support).[34]

In one of our small support test, we received an e-mail on the same day. The phone support is very friendly but was only available in English. For Skype chat, you just add as a contact via the link on the website of Twino and you can immediately start typing. So the help (if you need it at all) is always close by.

Secondary Market

Twino does not have a real secondary market like Bondora or Mintos. It is only possible to sell your investments (or parts of them). This is interesting, for example, if the loan has been extended by the borrower's possible extension of the loan, but you would like to get your money faster.

Handling is as straightforward as the rest of Twino's website. In addition to your investments already made, you have a "sell" button in which you enter and confirm a price. From this point on, your loan share is available for purchase. You can vary the price, but do not make a profit with it, such as Bondora, for example, since you can only raise the price to the amount of outstanding capital on this loan.

Our experiences with Twino

Twino is a very easy-to-use P2P platform, limited to the essentials, namely the investment. As the following screenshot reveals, one learns almost nothing about the borrower:

---

[34] Contact information can be found at
https://www.twino.eu/en/profile/investor/contacts

Example loan Twino

But if we are honest (and you will find out later), from an investor's point of view, it is not even necessary that you learn too much about the borrower, because the benefit of this information is quite low. Especially if you invest automatically, as we recommend.

Some investors are also very skeptical about the buyback guarantee, especially since Twino is supposed to buy back the loans after only 30 days. Our test confirms: It works perfectly and we have not heard of any other private investor. The overdue loans are bought back without any problems and the money is available for new investments.

We also like the Portfolio Builder from Twino very well. Similar to Mintos, here you have the possibility to activate several portfolio builders and to run strategies in parallel. However, the settings here are somewhat less extensive than with Mintos, which does not limit the purpose of the Portfolio Builder in any way:

Portfolio-Builder Twino

Basically, we think Twino is a great new and easy platform with many options and a decent return on investment. Especially the buyback guarantee makes the platform particularly attractive. If you're starting to invest money in P2P loans, Twino is a good first stop. Also for people who only want to park their money for a certain amount of time, Twino can be a good alternative. But you should always keep in mind that the borrower has the opportunity to extend his installments up to 6 months. A "payday loan" that only runs for one month can, therefore, be extended to a term of 7 months. If you do not want to, you have to intervene manually and offer your loan for sale.

The numbers are more than impressive despite the buyback guarantee, which sometimes reduces the rate of return, so this platform is a great alternative to other platforms. Being fully automated, Twino does not cost you a single minute a month, but even if you invest manually, it's faster than other platforms because you do not have too many decision-making criteria. Of course, you can also see this negatively, which we do not.

If you find Twino interesting, the easiest way to gain experience is to open an account and get started with a few bucks. We're pretty sure you like the platform. Try it.

10. INVESTLY

written by Claus Lehmann, publisher of
P2P-Banking.com & P2P-Kredite.com

General

Initially, Investly started lending to companies in 2014, and since the end of 2015, Investly has focused on invoice discounting. Investly is headquartered in London and has a branch in Tallinn.

In Investly's marketplace, investors are investing in receivables from invoices sold by small and medium-sized companies from Estonia and the UK. The advantage for the company is that they get the money immediately, instead of waiting for 30-120 days until the company they have supplied and billed for will pay according to the agreed payment term. Investors will then give a company a short-term loan until the supplier company pays.

Investly is a young platform, but it is growing strongly. The loan volume at the time of going to press was around EUR 1.1 million per month.[35] In the spring of 2018, Investly has raised over 600,000 pounds of new capital through an equity crowdfunding round to further develop the platform and has given business to these investors.[36]

The minimum amount for a primary market investment is 10 euros. According to the platform itself, the average return on investment is about 10.3% for Estonian loans and about 12.7% for UK loans. Currently, the platform is free for investors. Investly is funded by a fee of approximately 1.5%, which is charged from the company selling the bill "on top" on the lending rates that go to investors.

---

[35] https://www.p2p-banking.com/countries/germany-international-p2p-lending-volumes-january-2019/

[36] https://www.p2p-banking.com/sdrs/investly

Investly's website is easy to use. The user interface is completely available in English. Registration is just as easy as with the other international platforms. To start as an investor a short registration is required, followed by a deposit via bank transfer.

Security

Investly only finances invoices issued to companies that have been on the market for at least 3 years and generate at least 500,000 euros in sales per year. In addition, Investly collects credit information for both billers and bill recipients through a credit reference agency (Krediidiinfo AS) and displays them on the platform.

The rating expresses the creditworthiness and default risk, there are the following levels:
- AAA = excellent
- AA = very good
- A = good
- BBB = satisfactory
- BB = acceptable
- B = weak
- C = unsatisfactory; such companies are not accepted by Investly

Only invoices where the goods or services have already been delivered to the invoice recipient are financed by Investly, i.e no invoices will be paid for future services. In addition, Investly contacts the bill-to party and confirms that he has received the delivery and that he is satisfied with its execution.

In the invoice, the account to which the bill recipient is to pay is called the Investly account. The repayment of the loan is thus automatic, as soon as the bill recipient pays. Individual loans have additional collateral.

Loan default

Investly regularly publishes default rates. Currently, they were 1.01% in the UK market and 2.91% in the Estonian market (as of March 2018). Of these, debt collection has already recovered 90% of British and 10% of Estonian losses. Investly employs its own lawyer to track down failures.

Communications

Investly support is available via e-mail, phone and chat on the normal business hours (no 24-hour support). There is a dedicated employee responsible for investor support. He answers within a few hours.

Secondary market

Investly has no secondary market. However, this is not necessary because the maximum repayment term is 120 days (the average duration is only 31 days).

My experiences with Investly

Investly provides investors with a wealth of information about the bill and market activity to be financed.

Overview page of Investly

The most important information is the rating, that means the expected default risk of biller and bill-to party.

It is important to understand how the bidding works. Investly uses an auction period. This is stated and is often 24 or 48 hours. Investly mentions a maximum interest rate (eg 18%). In the bidding phase, all investors now bid - you can also make several different bids. If the sum of the bids exceeds the loan amount, then "Funding left 0.00" is at the top. The bids with the highest interest rate are then removed and the investors underbid each other. When the auction phase ends, all investors who are still in it receive the same interest rate as the highest still active bid.

Note the term of the loan. Some investors suspect that they will receive the mentioned percentage of interest on repayment. For example, at 100 € and 15.8% interest rate you expect 15.80 € interest. This is wrong, since the runtime is not one year, but, for example, 59 days. After 59 days the investor gets 59/365 * 15.8% * 100 €, that is 2.55 €.

At Investly, investors can either bid actively by hand or sit back and use the so-called "Autobidder" (Portfolio Builder).

Investly Autobidder

So far, I have only bid manually. Investly informs investors about large new loans by email. Small new loans are mostly completely filled by the auto-invest feature. Paradoxically, in parallel auctions, investors occasionally grant credit with a higher default risk at a lower final interest rate than the safer with better credit quality.[37]

As an investor, I was more likely to consider whether to use my funds to offer a loan with only a mediocre interest rate or to skip it and wait for a better interest rate - of course, my uninvested money would not by earning interest until then on the account.

It is also possible to finance British company invoices, which are then settled in pounds. I have not used this yet. Attention should then be paid to the resulting exchange rate risk and any bank charges incurred when depositing and paying out.

I'll continue to share my experiences with Investly on the P2P-Banking.com blog and the P2P Kredite forum.[38]

---

[37] https://www.p2p-kredite.com/diskussion/rationales-bietverhalten-t3958.html

[38] https://www.p2p-kredite.com/diskussion/investly-f24.html

11. ESTATEGURU
written by Claus Lehmann, publisher of
P2P-Banking.com & P2P-Kredite.com

General

Estateguru has been on the market since 2014. The platform provides loans secured by real estate and land to real estate developers in Estonia, Latvia, Lithuania and Finland. The head office of Estateguru is in Tallinn, Estonia.

The loans at Estateguru are for amounts between about 30,000 euros and 300,000 euros. The minimum bid for investors is 50 euros and is thus relatively high compared to other P2P credit platforms. Usual terms are 12 to 24 months, sometimes more.

Estateguru is also a young platform, but growth is clearly visible. The credit volume at the time of going to press was 6.5 million euros per month.[39]

According to the platform itself, the average return on investment is around 12.2%. The platform is free for investors. Estateguru is funded by fees charged to borrowers: 3-4% one-off and 0-2% annual fee.[40]

The website of Estateguru is very easy to use and provides detailed information about the loans. The user interface is available in both English and German. Registration is just as easy as with the other international platforms. To start as an investor a short registration is required, followed by a deposit via bank transfer.

---

[39] https://www.p2p-banking.com/tag/loan-volume/
[40] https://estateguru.co/faq/faq

Security

Each loan is secured by a mortgage. A distinction should be made between the 1st rank mortgage and the 2nd rank mortgage. Often, security is not the object for whose construction/development the loan is to be taken, but another building or property owned by the real estate developer.

Estateguru provides a security appraisal on the platform. The loan amount in relation to the value of the collateral results in the LTV of, for example, 65%. The higher the LTV, the higher the risk in case of default.

Loan default

There were only a few defaults at Estateguru. Most have been recovered so far. If there are delays in payment, Estateguru will try to find a solution together with the borrower. For example, a temporary suspension of repayment is possible. If no solution is found, Estateguru will hire a law firm to collect the claim. If necessary, this can force the sale of collateral via a foreclosure sale. If the proceeds of this sale are below the loan amount, there will be a partial default on the investors (therefore the LTV is important).

Communications

Estateguru support is available by email and by phone during normal business hours (no 24-hour support).

Secondary market

Currently, there is no secondary market. As an investor, you have to hold loans until the end of the term.

My experiences with Estateguru

Estateguru provides investors with detailed information about the loan. These include photos, valuations, security status, a link to the land registry, which is kept digital in Estonia, and information about the borrower. Also, of course, credit information and the payment plan.

Example loan Estateguru

Basically, the repayment takes place in a sum at the end (not monthly). For some loans, the interest is paid monthly, for others, bullet loans with payment at the end (you find this information in the description).

Usual interest rates are between approx. 10% and 12%. At Estateguru, investors can invest manually or through auto-investment. For small bids, there is only a very simple auto-invest, only from a bid level of at least 250 euros, investors can make a detailed selection on "select criteria". Estateguru sends a notification email as soon as a new loan has been listed on the platform. Theoretically, this is then open for a bidding time of, for example, 3 days. However, since new loans (at least smaller ones) in practice are filled within a few hours by bids, investors often keep assets in the account, even if it is, of course, not interest-free, as long as it is not invested.

Several of my loans have already been repaid. Most of the rest is going according to plan, some with smaller delays. My portfolio list shows me a return of 11.54%.

For my portfolio, I chose rather short-term loans from Estonia, mainly with monthly interest payments, and otherwise simply put on diversification, and did not deal with the valuation reports.

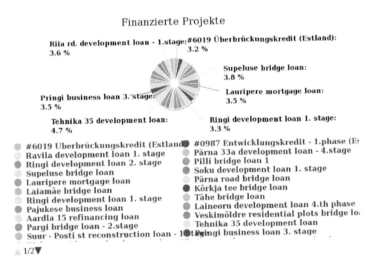

Pie chart of my portfolio - no credit accounts for more than 5% of my portfolio

Tip: Investors wishing to sign up for another investor will receive from Estateguru 0.5% bonus on all investments during the first 90 days of sign-up (credited after the loan has been created).[41]

I continue to report on my experience with Estateguru on the P2P-Banking.com blog and the P2P Kredite Forum.[42]

---

[41] Cashback valid at the time of going to press; Bonus promotion can be terminated or changed by Estateguru all the time.
https://www.p2p-banking.com/p2p-lending-cashback-bonus/
[42] https://www.p2p-kredite.com/diskussion/estateguru-f23.html

12. VIVENTOR

General

Viventor has been around since the beginning of 2016 and the platform is based in Latvia's Riga. As with many other platforms from this region, it is still a very young startup. Viventor is, however, a subsidiary of the Spanish company Prestamos Prima.[43]

The platform started with secured real estate loans, meanwhile, also simple consumer loans are being offered on the marketplace. As with Mintos, Viventor does not lend itself, but uses external lenders, the so-called loan originators.

This fact also brings the same advantages that Mintos can claim for themselves. At the time of writing, investments were made via Viventor in Bulgaria, Spain, Poland, Kenya and the Netherlands.

All loans are already pre-financed, which means that there are no waiting times like Crosslend or Auxmoney, but you can invest directly. Also, cancellations do not exist. Viventor is open to investors from all over Europe and currently many loans are backed by the buyback guarantee.

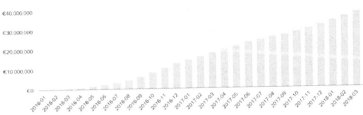

Growth of Viventor over the years

---

[43] Further information about parent company under
https://www.prestamosprima.com

Viventor has grown over the years to a moderately large platform that, while not able to keep up with the volume of Mintos, but still does not have to hide from other platforms. Most Viventor investors have an average return of 11-12%. As always, the platform is free for you as an investor and you can start your investment from 10 EUR per loan.

The website of the platform is simple and tidy, but unfortunately only available in English. Initially, Viventor had a German translation, but this was so bad that it had to be taken offline to avoid misunderstandings.

Security and loan default

Like some other platforms, Viventor is part of a larger enterprise network. So it is unlikely that the website will be gone in no time. Actually, the platform at the time of writing this book is already almost 3 years old. In addition, as mentioned above, Viventor does not lend itself, but only provides the platform for external loan suppliers. The platform risk is, therefore, more than manageable.

The loans themselves are very often secured with the buyback guarantee, which will be repurchased after 30, 60 or 90 days (depending on the loan originator). In addition, there is a so-called payment guarantee, which also offers the platform Twino. In this case, the loan originator jumps in to cover the payments but does not buy back the loan. Loan originators are still required to have "Skin in the Game". That means nothing else than that they must have financed 5% of the credit themselves to be in the same position as the investor.

Since Viventor offers so many collaterals for the investor, you do not get anything from a possible collection process. Only with an unsecured mortgage and business loans, the borrower must provide additional security, which is usually a piece of land. However, to this day we have not experienced any losses on Viventor.

Communications

German investors need to be strong on this platform. What begins on the website continues in communication. Viventor offers no

German support. For us personally, this should never be a reason against an investment. If you cannot do it, learn it. This applies to many things in life and thus also to languages. Apart from the linguistic difference, Viventor's support has been very helpful and competent to us and is in no way inferior to other platforms.

Secondary market

Viventor also offers a secondary market where it is possible to buy shares of other investors and sell yours. There are no costs for you on this platform, so you can make one or two bargains at no extra charge, if you want to spend the time. Because bargain search is as often called manual investment. On platforms like Bondora, you can also automatically invest in the secondary market, but this is not (yet) possible on Viventor.

The use of the secondary market is extremely easy. In addition to your investments, you have a sell button, where you can enter your discount and confirm the offer. Then your loan lands on the secondary market and depending on the discount you have given, you will soon find a buyer for it.

Portfolio-Builder

Viventor relies on automated investment. Although you can also invest manually on the platform, we do not recommend it to you. Take advantage of the opportunities available to you to make the most of your resources.

The Viventor Portfolio-Builder

The Portfolio Builder is very quickly configured and you can start the investment immediately. At Viventor, you can run multiple portfolio builders on multiple strategies in parallel. This can be useful if you want to test investment strategies or pursue several different strategies.

Our experiences with Viventor

Unfortunately, Kolja has not invested in Viventor, but I've been here since the beginning of 2016 and since then I write reviews about the platform, which you can read on my blog.[44]

At first my experiences were very mixed. The catastrophic German translation coupled with poor credit availability (even with small sums of money) was not much fun. But unlike many P2P investors, I never leave a platform just because my money is lying around uninvested for a few weeks or months. Therefore, I only stopped my money transfer order for the platform, because I knew that most of the time, the offer will eventually pick up and you are fully invested. That was exactly the case with Viventor.

Since about the end of 2017, new loan originators have come to the platform, the website has been overhauled, but the German translation switched off. My money transfer order has also been reactivated and the result is impressive:

---

[44] You can read all about the reports at https://passives-einkommen-mit-p2p.de/category/viventor/

ALL TIME TRANSACTIONS			
Funds invested	€4'250.00	Investments made	425
Principal repaid	€3'527.13	Loans repaid	352
Interest received	€23.73	Loans sold on Secondary Market	0
Late fee received	€17.45	Loan parts currently held	73
Rate of return (XIRR)	10.93%		

My investments at Viventor

With currently 10.93%, I am just below the average return of most P2P investors, which is because in 2016, I still had a very unfortunate configured auto-invest to get any loans at all.

I can absolutely recommend the platform at the editorial deadline of this book as an alternative to a giant like Mintos or very small platforms like Robocash. As more and more loan originators get onto the platform, as an investor you can diversify your portfolio, which will ensure a stable investment in the future.

13. VIAINVEST

General

Viainvest is a very interesting platform from - how could it be otherwise - Riga in Latvia. The platform started providing online loans in November 2016 and we have been gaining experience there ever since. However, Viainvest is a bit different from the competition, as it is only a platform from the outside. Behind the loans and Viainvest itself is the VIA SMS Group[45], lending in many European countries and putting them online on the Viainvest platform.

By contrast, the Via SMS Group has existed since 2008, so you cannot really talk about a brand new platform at Viainvest because they already have a lot of experience.

Operating areas of the Via SMS Group

The loans you can currently invest in on Viainvest are limited entirely

---

[45] Further information can be read under http://viasmsgroup.com/

to pre-funded short-term consumer loans through 4 in-house loan lenders from Poland, Spain, the Czech Republic and Lithuania. In the next time, they will also add Sweden. The other countries in which the parent company operates are currently not affiliated with the online procurement model.

Loans on Viainvest are also covered by the buyback guarantee, so you cannot make any losses here under the best of conditions. You can act as an investor from any European country and make your investments starting from a sum of 10 EUR per loan. The platform looks very tidy and is easy to use.

Communications

Communication with Viainvest is extremely good across all channels offered. Even with Skype, you can communicate with the support, which of course, is pleasant. Until recently, they even had a German support staff who answered all requests in German. Viainvest always takes direct care of the investors and also implements suggestions for improvement.

Security and loan default

The greatest security of Viainvest is also the parent company, which controls the allocation internally. When we visited Viainvest in 2018, we also felt we knew what they were doing here. The other non-affiliated countries are not available to investors for a good reason: the managers of Viainvest explained to us that in the event of a failure of the repurchase guarantee, the investor's money can be secured. So they will only accept additional loan lenders if they are absolutely sure about the risk calculations.

As just mentioned, the loans are fully covered by the buyback guarantee. Although there is the option in the Portfolio Builder to deselect them, there is no offer without a buyback guarantee at the time of writing this book. Which, however, as with other platforms with repurchase guarantee means that you cannot follow the collection process if a loan defaulted.

Secondary market

At the time of publication of this book, there is no secondary market on Viainvest. However, as you can see on other platforms, this is a very popular tool, which means that we may eventually see it on the platform.

Portfolio-Builder

Automatic investing is also possible on Viainvest and is also the preferred option by many investors. The Portfolio Builder is very easy to use and starts directly with the investment.

Viainvest Portfolio Builder

However, you cannot set up much here, but this is not necessary with the loan offer on Viainvest.

Our experiences with Viainvest

Viainvest is currently the only platform known to us that levies withholding taxes directly. You can protect yourself against this by issuing a so-called "tax identity certificate "from the Federal Central Tax Office, which you must have previously completed by your tax office. The whole process must be done once a year, as the certificate is only valid for one year. It's a standard process done relatively quickly, so the effort is fine.

The problem here, however, is that this statement does not apply to Polish loans! So that means you always pay withholding tax on investments in Poland. Unfortunately, you do not come around here. This, of course, makes Polish loans extremely unattractive, which is why we recommend removing them directly from the Portfolio Builder.

Why is Viainvest doing that? This was explained by the contact persons of the platform when we were in Riga. In Latvia, there are currently guidelines on how to handle P2P loans from the platforms and Viainvest is very strict about it and they believe they are doing it right. On the other hand, that means that many other platforms currently interpret the policy differently. If the requirements become law and other platforms have to follow, Viainvest was already on the right track. It will be interesting to see what happens here in 2018/2019.

Apart from tax issues, Viainvest is a forward-looking company, as evidenced by the last-introduced product "Cryptoloans [46]"with which Viainvest wants to link the P2P concept to the blockchain. The product is currently only available in Sweden, but we are watching it with excitement! All in all, and since the loans are almost all short-term anyway, Viainvest is worth an investment.

[46] Further information can be found at:
https://www.cryptoloan.se/en/

14. BASIC INFORMATION ON INVESTING FROM EXPERIENCES

As an introduction to our experiences on topics such as diversification, portfolio builders, etc., we wanted to pass on a few general tips on investments, which are mostly tailored to P2P platforms, but many of them are also for any other investment. Let's start with a quote from Benjamin Franklin:[47]

> *" Human bliss is not so much determined by great happy events that are very rare, but by small benefits that are quite commonplace."*

With this in mind, be aware of the following twelve points as often as possible to get maximum insights and benefits:

1. No investment is safe! If you think you can invest your money 100% safely in any form of investment, we recommend that you read some basic literature on investing.[48] Especially P2P loans with enormous yield spreads can be loss-making - buyback guarantee or not.

2. Your investments in individual loans should be kept emotionless. So avoid looking every day for earned interest or buybacks.

3. Never invest your "last shirt". Approximately 25% of your total assets should always be available as cash reserves, so that you can respond firstly to investment opportunities, and secondly, you do not have to sell any investments if you urgently need private money (if you lose your job for example). Of course, this safety cushion can vary according to personal expenses, but it should never be less than 3-6 net monthly salaries. You should

---

[47] Printer, Publisher, Writer, Scientist, Inventor and statesman (Founding Father of the USA).
[48] See recommended reading

always be able to bridge this number of months without income without having to sell your investments. In the case of P2P loans, as you have seen, selling will be difficult anyway. Here is just the possibility to phase out current loans or to sell on the secondary market, if this exists on your chosen P2P platform.

4. Always keep your eyes and ears open for new investments or improvement techniques. Is there, for example, a new P2P provider on the market? Do they use revolutionary techniques? Are there special investment techniques from other areas that you can map to P2P? A good starting point for such things is, for example, our P2P community on Facebook.[49]

5. Always act from your own opinion in your decisions and do not let others influence you (not even us). So you also carry the responsibility yourself. And let's be honest, you have to end up anyway.

6. Diversify your loans properly to protect your assets from total loss. How exactly you do that, you'll learn in the other chapters.

7. Believe in the platform you use. If you're always unsure, you emotionally attach to things that you cannot change in the end. If you do not trust the provider, just let the loans run out and use another platform on the market. Offers are enough there, because, in addition to the P2P platforms presented here, there are countless others that you can use for your investments.

8. Understand the possibilities provided by your used P2P lending platform and use them. Do you don't understand them, do not use them. This is especially true for the foreign-language platforms, as misunderstandings happen faster.

---

[49] Our community you will find under
https://www.facebook.com/groups/p2pcommunity/

---

9. Have fun investing and building motivation so you can stick with it when things are not going so well. Motivations can be financial independence and security, holiday travel or even just rising passive payments.

10. Try to learn from experienced P2P investors (from books and forums), but always scrutinize their views and methods and decide on your own. This also applies to the book in front of you.

11. Always stay realistic and always appreciate your investment realistically. You will not become a millionaire in a short time with P2P loans alone. Building a safe, well-diversified portfolio and the necessary know-how will take years.

12. Keep track of your loans and do not invest too quickly in too many projects on initial euphoria, but use the first few months to perhaps invest in just a few projects. With this, you gain experience and get started, for example, with the withdrawal procedures and many other things about your p2p platforms.

15. DIVERSIFICATION

Before we look at our diversification strategies, let's, first of all, take a moment to think about what "diversification" means and what this is all about in detail. "Diversification" in Germany is officially defined in the dictionary as "change, variety or diversity".[50] And that's exactly what it is in the financial world. By investing in the P2P sector in addition to your stocks or other asset classes, you have already diversified, for example, equities typically do not correlate or are not heavily correlated with loans, unless you are assisting someone who wants to buy shares from his loan. The P2P system should be diversified classically like a larger equity portfolio.

When it comes to P2P investments, diversification can mean two things. First, diversification of your funds across multiple platforms. We then talk about the so-called "platform diversification". A P2P platform is an economic company and can bankrupt. Even if your loans continue to run in the background, this condition is a very unpleasant situation.

Perhaps some still remember the Icelandic Kaupthing Edge Bank[51] in the financial crisis. They lured with incredibly high overnight interest rates (even for the level at this time) and just under 34,000 savers fell for it and parked there a lot of money. One morning, with these 34,000 savers, the accounts suddenly became inaccessible and the money completely in abeyance. At that time, it was completely unclear whether the funds could be repaid and the process took months. To cap it all, the funds were hedged up to just under 20,000 euros and some had deliberately invested much more in the Kaupthing Edge. Luckily everything went with a happy ending for the savers.

---

[50] The exact word definition is to be found under
http://www.duden.de/rechtschreibung/Diversifikation
[51] further information about Kaupthing Bank you will find here:
https://en.wikipedia.org/wiki/Kaupthing_Bank

Although it seems a lot less critical on P2P platforms because of the backup concepts, you do not want to experience that feeling. Therefore, you should not just place your investments on a single platform. Of course, it makes no sense to go with 20 euros, which you can invest in a month, with 4 different platforms at the start, but you should spread from a certain portfolio size on multiple platforms.

Second, you can spread on loan level. Diversification, therefore, means that funds are not fully invested in a single loan but are distributed among different loans. Important to note here is that you do not mindlessly invest with random mini amounts, but act with head and brain. Exaggerated diversification only increases the effort; clever diversification secures capital and facilitates the overview. In the picture below, you can see the effect of diversification on the final return of an investor. This statistic was provided by the American provider Lending Club[52], should, however, in our opinion be well transferred to any P2P platform:

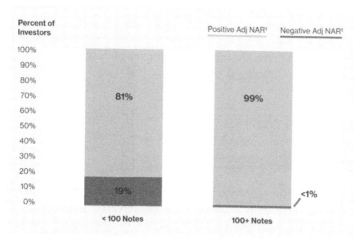

Risk reduction through diversification

---

[52] Further information of the provider LendingClub.com on diversification, you can find under
https://www.lendingclub.com/public/diversification.action

So, the higher your degree of diversification is, the less likely it is to lose total. So to give you a small roadmap for your investments that you can reach these levels of diversification, we have developed two simple strategies for you that you can use yourself and build on your investments from the start. As simple as they are, it's very important to understand them because that's where most of the security of your portfolio is based. So before we begin to diversify, we need to set our diversification strategy or degree of diversification so that we know at all times how to invest to diversify safely.

Strategy 1: "Start free"

As a guideline, we specify a portfolio diversification of at least 40 loan projects, which corresponds to a diversification of 2.5%. This value has no scientific background but is based on simplicity for the start of the portfolio and our experience. You can also prove your degree of diversification with other values, but both strategies will work anyway. Let's take a look at a starter portfolio, which is still at 0 Euro. The first goal should be that we want to invest 1,000 euros. We now always invest 2.5% of our target portfolio, which in our case amounts to 25 euros per loan. 25 euros are often the minimum investment amount of many P2P providers (especially in Germany), which is why we have chosen this starting value. Ideally, we would have spread our default risk to 40 loans when we reached the 1,000 euros.

Target portfolio: 1.000 EUR
Investment per loan: 1.000 EUR * 0,025 = 25 EUR
Diversification: 40 loan projects to 1.000 EUR

Once you reach the target portfolio, you set yourself a new goal. This goal can be completely arbitrary and will have no impact on the strategy. In our example, we set ourselves the next goal a higher investment sum, for example, 2,000 euros. Our investment is now 50 euros per loan:

Current Portfolio: 1.000 EUR
Target portfolio: 2.000 EUR
Investment per loan: 2.000 EUR * 0,025 = 50 EUR
Diversification: 40 loan projects to 2.000 EUR

Your risk in the growth phase is now spread over more than 40 loan projects. These loans expire over time and the investment amount per loan is replaced by the newly calculated investment amount, so you have always diversified your portfolio with this strategy to at least 40 loan projects (probably more). If you already have a current loan portfolio, that's no problem either. Because loans, as just mentioned, eventually expire, you can just take over the strategy. Let's take a look at a freely chosen example:

Current portfolio: 7.513 EUR
Target portfolio: 10.000 EUR
Investment per loan: 10.000 EUR * 0,025 = 250 EUR
Diversification: 40 loan projects to 10.000 EUR

As a general warning, however, is on the way given that the diversification is not a miracle cure. Again, it can hail losses, but it greatly reduces the likelihood of total loss, so you should rely on healthy diversification for P2P loans as well. Furthermore, you should always choose quickly achievable goals, so as to build up your diversification meaningful. If you start at 0 Euro, we would not recommend setting your target portfolio immediately to 50,000 Euro. In general, that's because we recommend Strategy 1 only as a start. In the long run, this level of diversification is too low and you should quickly move to number 2 or later diversify more.

Strategy 2: "Build security"

An almost identical strategy is our second proposal. Here we pay a predetermined amount on our P2P platform and invest only 1% of the total. The difference is, therefore, only in the degree of diversification, which leads to a higher number of loans and may not initially be applicable to every P2P platform due to the minimum contribution. Therefore, it makes sense to start with Strategy 1 and eventually change to Strategy 2.

Available capital: 1.000 EUR
Investment per loan: 1.000 EUR * 0, 01 = 10 EUR
Diversification: 100 loan projects to 1.000 EUR

Once we have invested all our available capital, we will pay and determine the new investment amount based on the percentage:

> Current portfolio: 1.000 EUR
> Available capital: 1.000 EUR
> Investment per loan: 2.000 EUR $* 0,01 = 20$ EUR
> Diversification: 100 loan projects to 2.000 EUR

With this method, you reduce the risk of default to an absolute minimum and rarely manage more than 150 loan projects. Here too, as in Strategy 1, the effect is that, despite the grant of new capital, old loans continue to run for the time being, even if they are based on a different calculation basis. In our opinion, you should go even deeper into diversification, even if the overview suffers from the high number of loans at some point. But safety is more important at this point. Based on the two examples, you can easily develop your own strategies for even deeper diversification. The calculation principle is always the same.

According to an article by "Börse online" Lending Club sees a P2P investment as sufficiently diversified only from 250 - 300 loans.[53] However, this recommendation served to show that even with high-risk credit ratings and sufficient diversification, one can generate a good return. When the first edition of our guide appeared in October 2015, we did not recommend it, but with today's experience, we say that the more diversified you can do the better.

With tools like the Portfolio Builder, this is no longer a problem today. Whether you diversify to 100 or 1000 loans does not matter. We both have for example, over 1000 active loans on the Bondora platform. But in the case of a series of outages, this could be a decisive advantage.

---

[53] http://www.boerse-online.de/nachrichten/meinungen/Taugen-P2P-Kredite-als-Anlageklasse-1000528693/3

This is underlined by a study by the Lend Academy[54], which we evaluated, with US investors being the most successful, diversifying their portfolio to around 800 loans. Ultimately, however, you alone decide on your level of diversification. If you follow our strategies, you will have basic diversification in your portfolio and be able to build on that later.

However, you should leave the fingers of excessive diversification if you invest manually. Because here you lose the overview quickly and also a lot of time. Manually diversifying to several hundred loans no longer has much to do with investing but would be a day-to-day hobby.

---

[54] https://passives-einkommen-mit-p2p.de/wieviel-diversifikation-ist-genug-bei-p2p-krediten/

16. CALCULATE RIGHT YIELDS WITH THE XIRR FUNCTION

Now that we have set strategies and a roadmap, the next step is to control our investment. If you are a bit more familiar with the P2P market and have invested in multiple marketplaces, you will find out that all platforms show you the performance of your current portfolio. In theory, this sounds great, except that there is a problem: Each platform has its own method of calculating the performance, so you do not know which one is really accurate and which one is not. Here are a few examples:

The german platform Auxmoney, for example, calculates a return index.[55] This is based on a formula that calculates the interest paid by the borrower on a monthly basis and the investor fee and puts it in relation to the outstanding repayment of the loan. The whole thing looks like this:

$$RI_n = \left(\frac{\sum_{k=1}^{n} \text{Zinsen}_k - \text{Anlegergebühr} - \text{ggf. geschätzter Ausfall}}{\sum_{k=0}^{n-1} \text{offene Tilgung}_k} + 1 \right)^{12} - 1$$

Return index from Auxmoney

Mintos, in turn, calculates the so-called NAR[56], which stands for Net Annualized Return. The NAR is determined on the basis of the extended internal rate of return[57] (XIRR), but other factors also flow in here.

---

[55] For more information on the return calculation at Auxmoney, please visit: https://www.auxmoney.com/kredit/info/anleger-info.html
[56] You can read how the NAR is calculated on the Mintos website: https://help.mintos.com/hc/en-us/articles/115002853149-What-is-net-annualised-return-NAR-
[57] Further information on the internal rate of return: https://de.wikipedia.org/wiki/Interner_Zinsfu%C3%9F

Bondora now actually calculates the average annual return using the extended internal rate of return based on the following data: time and amount of investments, time and amount of repayments, and present net worth of the portfolio.[58] But even here, other factors are included in the calculation, such. For example, overdue loans.

So it's high time to learn to use another tool to control your P2P investment and normalize your return calculation. Bondora is already quite close to it, even if overdue loans totally distort the result in the end. Also, we use the already mentioned XIRR function, but the classic version, in which no extras flow in, which distort the return calculation.

In principle, it is very simple and if you do it from the beginning, it is an effort of maybe 5 minutes each month. All you need is the following things:

1. Your exact deposits and withdrawals on your marketplace with date
2. Your current account balance

The determination of this data is usually relatively easy. But it's best to briefly show you through the Mintos portfolio. In most cases, you can read the current portfolio balance directly on the start page or your investor dashboard (at least that's the case with Mintos). In order to get more detailed information, you must retrieve your bank statements via the top menu bar.

Then you simply choose a start and an end date of the investigation. Note that you need all deposits and withdrawals. So select your entire registration period from your platform. Next, you go in the case of Mintos on the selection box "payment method" and select the item "incoming payments from the bank account".

---

[58] Here you can find the method of calculating the net yield of the Bondora platform: https://support.bondora.com/hc/en-us/articles/214230845-How-do-we-calculate-net-return-

Kontoauszug

Anfangsdatum	Enddatum	Zahlungsart	
01.12.2015	18.08.2016	Eingehende Zahlungen vom Bankkonto	Auswählen

Heute Gestern Diese Woche Dieser Monat Letzte Woche Letzter Monat Letzter Monat und dieser Monat

Zusammenfassender Auszug
Eingehende Zahlungen vom Bankkonto

Datum	Einzelheiten	Umsatz
08.12.2015	Transaction ID 103441487 - Eingehende Zahlungen vom Bankkonto	164.66
08.01.2016	Transaction ID 103441550 - Eingehende Zahlungen vom Bankkonto	244.60
20.01.2016	Transaction ID 103441622 - Eingehende Zahlungen vom Bankkonto	271.99
17.02.2016	Transaction ID 103441782 - Eingehende Zahlungen vom Bankkonto	201.35
15.03.2016	Transaction ID 103442317 - Eingehende Zahlungen vom Bankkonto	204.18
15.04.2016	Transaction ID 104549526 - Eingehende Zahlungen vom Bankkonto	181.18
28.06.2016	Transaction ID 106146959 - Eingehende Zahlungen vom Bankkonto	300.00
27.07.2016	Transaction ID 109987209 - Eingehende Zahlungen vom Bankkonto	243.43

Account statement Mintos

Now that you have all the values, you have two options. You can either use one of the simple XIRR online calculators or build your own Excel spreadsheet. For example, as an online calculator, you can use Simon Cunningham's LendingMemo page.[59] The handling is actually self-explanatory. Currently, as far as we know, no computer supports the possibility of downloading the results. This means you have to laboriously re-enter the results each time you want to recalculate your return.

So if you have already made several deposits and may have been in the subject for several years, the other alternative is for you, namely the manual calculation in Excel or another spreadsheet program of your choice. Here you simply transfer your values, just like with the XIRR online computers. Just keep in your table according to the following picture in our simple example:

---

[59] https://www.lendingmemo.com/xirr-calculator/

	A	B
1	Datum	Betrag
2	08.12.2015	164,66 €
3	08.01.2016	244,60 €
4	20.01.2016	271,99 €
5	17.02.2016	291,35 €
6	16.03.2016	204,18 €
7	15.04.2016	181,18 €
8	28.06.2016	300,00 €
9	27.07.2016	243,43 €
10	**18.08.2016**	- 1.985,00 €
11	**XIRR**	11,10%

XIRR-Table in Microsoft Excel

In column A you put the data of the deposit, in column B the corresponding amount. It is important here that deposits are given as a positive value and payments as a negative value. Finally, you also enter your current account balance with the date and negative value. Then you can use this formula to calculate the real return:

```
=XINTZINSFUSS(B2:B10;A2:A10)
```

XIRR-Formula

Please keep in mind that the XIRR calculation is really meaningful only after about one year of running time, so the numbers will be very different from those of the platforms in the beginning. Another benefit of using your own XIRR calculation is that you can easily use it for other types of investments, such as: For your ETFs or stocks. These easy and simple means allows you to optimally monitor and, if necessary, adjust your passive income streams from investment sources, should this ever be necessary.

Incidentally, it is also more comfortable with the freeware Portfolio Performance. Here you can keep track of all your interest income in a clear and structured way for years to come. You can find detailed instructions on my blog.[60]

---

[60] https://passives-einkommen-mit-p2p.de/portfolio-performance-wie-du-deine-p2p-plattformen-einfach-verwalten-kannst/

17. LONG- OR SHORT-TERM LOANS?

At our next topic, many will think at first glance that it makes no difference whether to invest in long or short term loans; at most a personal one. But we will briefly describe why that is not the whole truth.

Short-term loans have the following advantages in our eyes: For short-term investors, the return flow rate is logically very high compared to long-term loans and, therefore, it significantly improves the monthly repayment of a P2P platform. However, if you want to invest in the long term, this effect is at most a psychological or emotional benefit. But since we invest without emotion, we should skip this advantage mentally. Logically, short-term loans with high rates are more likely to be used by people who only need short-term debt financing, and, therefore, the likelihood of premature loan repayment is higher than long-term loans.

For example, if you want to park your money only for a short time because you need it in the foreseeable future, the short runners are a great choice and you should bet on platforms that either only offer these loans or configure your Portfolio Builder to do so. From our point of view, these are mainly the platforms Twino, Mintos, Viainvest and Viventor.

Let's look at the long-term loans. With a lasting investment in the P2P market, our motto is: "The longer the credit, the higher the benefits." The longer the loan runs, the longer the capital is tied up. Ostensibly a strange argument, but a longer term, on the other hand, means no idle time. When a loan expires, you have to invest the money again, which is not always easy, as long as you're on the move with a lot of capital, because the investor market is growing rapidly and the marketplaces are contested. Especially when you invest manually, it can take an incredible amount of time to constantly refinance your returns. With long-term loans, you can significantly reduce this effect.

There is also another advantage, but it is provider specific. It is all about P2P platforms where you can sell investments in a secondary market, such as: Bondora; a platform which, according to this book, will surely be an option for every P2P investor. Exactly this possibility with Bondora can make a big difference, if one consciously uses it and remembers it. For example, if you want to sell an overdue loan that only has 9 months remaining, the expected value is less than an overdue loan that runs for 48 months. In addition to the interest rate, the expected value at Bondora influences the resale transaction fee. Because of this fact, long-term loans are much better off here again.

If you have little time for your investments, it makes less sense to invest in short-term investors. However, if it's your hobby and you enjoy rolling, analyzing and estimating loans all day long, then just go ahead! From time to time, manual investing can actually be fun and bring a few new insights here and there that you no longer notice when you look into your depot only once a month or even less frequently. Apart from that, it automatically makes you have to deal with the platform. Ultimately, however, it depends on your personal situation and your preferences as to which loans you prefer. We both prefer to invest in the long term because we do not need the payouts.

18. PORTFOLIO-BUILDER

Let's be honest: As an investor in P2P markets, our focus is on stable and easily achievable returns in the shortest possible time. We don't know anything about you, but we don't want to spend half a day in front of the computer checking the latest credit offers for sense and social background. If we can take these aspects with us, that's a nice thing, but that's not why we're here. We want to invest our money profitably and build up a passive income with it at best.

Minimum time expenditure with maximum return should be our goal, so that we can put our spare time again into new projects, books or simply into ourselves. To make things easier, some P2P platforms have developed so-called portfolio builders. Do not be fooled by the name. Sometimes they are also called investment agents, automatic investing, auto-invest, auto bidder or otherwise. Here in this book, we call this technique "portfolio builder", based on the (well-known) Auxmoney platform in Germany. Basically, it's your personal employee who works for you 24 hours, never gets tired or sick, does not go to the works council, because he's overworked and does not ask for salary increases.

The portfolio builders should make your life easier and invest the money in various loan projects for you according to your pre-set requirements. These presets look different on every platform and it's up to you to define them. With some, you can only pretend the sum that you want to invest and in some others, you can play around in the smallest detail of the settings. We advise you to try to make the most important configurations, but not to bother with them in detail, as this will ultimately make you need to constantly work on controlling your portfolio builder and perfecting the settings.

However, to help you understand the key things that you can use to configure your personal portfolio builder, we've identified three, we think, important criteria that you should always consider (if your P2P platform has a portfolio builder with those functions). These are the following:

1. **The solvency.** This not only determines a large part of the credit selection but also reflects your personal risk profile. The better the credit ratings, the more stable your returns; the worse the credit ratings, the more volatile your portfolio, but the higher your returns in case of doubt. Simplified visualized, the whole thing looks like this:

Risk classification of the solvency[61]

However, this criterion is not applicable to every platform. Some platforms, for example, have no credit rating system that you could pay attention to.

2. **The investment sum of the portfolio.** This determines how much you want to give your money into strange hands. Initially, we recommend you trade conservatively and start with smaller totals for configuration purposes to get a feel for your portfolio builder.

3. **The investment amount per loan.** Remember the chapter of Diversification! Take this philosophy into your portfolio builder as well and have it diligently diversify for you, but please on such a scale that you do not completely lose track. Therefore, before deciding on the investment amount per loan, we recommend that you read through the chapter on diversification and internalize it again.

---

[61] Risk scale from the article "Impact of the new Bondora.com Rating System" from www.moneyisyourfriend.eu

Furthermore, you should be aware that it may take a while with the Portfolio Builder until the appropriate portfolio is distributed. For example, if you only invest in loans of the highest credit quality, it can happen to you on some platforms that you hardly get any offers there. Therefore, it is best to have a healthy distribution right at the beginning to make sure that the Portfolio Builder is working properly. But above all, be patient and do not look into your portfolio every 5 minutes to see if your portfolio builder has already invested in a new loan. Check with deposits, however, whether your investment goal still fits. Because if the balance of your virtual investment account exceeds your set investment goal, the Portfolio Builder will not invest, and you'll be unnecessarily troubleshooting.

At the beginning (if you're launching a platform), we recommend looking at a defined time of day every day and gradually reducing that rhythm to once a month, as long as you're sure your Portfolio Builder is working properly. By achieving this goal, you have built a (hopefully) emotionless, scalable and automated investment system.

19. SECONDARY MARKET

written by Andreas Tielmann. Publisher of
P2P-Anlage.de

While in a normal credit marketplace, the loans are still "fresh", so no installments have been repaid, there are already older loans from other investors in the secondary market, which offer them for sale. The secondary market makes it possible for investors to trade among themselves with individual loans, which otherwise have a fixed term. Without a secondary market, you are bound to the entire term and cannot be separated from the loans before. If there is a secondary market, there is the possibility of offering your own loans for sale to other investors.

Advantages for buyers

You can buy loans for which several installments have already been paid. If only a few loans are available in the normal marketplace, you can quickly build up a broader portfolio in the secondary market by purchasing already-existing loans from other investors.

Advantages for Sellers

There is the possibility, if needed, of quickly getting liquidity. So you can set single or multiple loans for sale and not the full term is tied to a loan. So you can also, for example, offer loans that run for 5 years, even if you do not want to keep them for so long. These are put up for sale according to their own maximum desired maturity on the secondary market and then receive the remaining nominal value.

Disadvantages of using a secondary market

The secondary market does not only have advantages for the investor, on the contrary, it also has some disadvantages that you should not ignore.

- Loss of time: Although each secondary market works similarly, it takes time to understand all the details and the process.

- No sale is guaranteed. If there is no buyer, the price must be changed several times until a successful transaction occurs.

- There is a risk, especially among beginners, of offering loans too cheaply.

- Often a secondary market is full of overpriced offers, as the best and cheapest offers are already bought quickly and only the overpriced ones are left over. As a brand new investor, with no experience buying loans on the secondary market, it is not recommended to use this feature.

Especially if you want to switch to other P2P platforms or other asset classes, the secondary market can be very useful. Although you usually already receive the monthly installments, it may take a long time before you get back a majority of the investment. Each loan has a current nominal value that can be taken as a reference. That's the remaining balance that the borrower still has to pay.

If a borrower already has multiple on-time installments, other investors are often willing to pay a higher price than the face value. Because here, the borrower has already proven his good payment history.

On the other hand, if the borrower is experiencing financial difficulties, a discount to the nominal value must be offered as there is an increased credit default risk. In this case, a loan is sold cheaper than the remaining repayment value. The amount of discounts varies depending on the type of loan:

- The highest discounts available are for loans that are unsecured and no repurchase guarantee, such as at Bondora for example. Here are the deductions even up to 85%. This means in plain text that the seller no longer expects many payments and wants to sell the loan almost completely at a loss.

- Lower are the discounts offered on secured loans. Because if it comes to financial difficulties, just the secured object, for example, a property sold in extreme cases and the proceeds paid to investors.

- The lowest are the discounts offered on credit marketplaces with a buyback guarantee, such as Mintos for example. Since the lenders themselves repurchase the loans at their nominal value, it makes little sense to sell secured loans at a discount.

Example (with buyback guarantee)

If a buyback guarantee exists, there are usually few price fluctuations. Because the credit default risk is borne by the platform or the credit issuer. Here, the discounts are so very limited, since it is guaranteed to receive the nominal price after a certain time (depending on the platform 30-60 days). Nevertheless, mark-ups on the nominal value can be achieved if punctual installments have been paid for several months.

Example (without buyback guarantee)

Credit share 50 euros. After 6 paid installments, the borrower has already paid 10 euros. The nominal value of the loan is, therefore, still 40 euros. If so far all the installments have been paid on time, other investors are willing to pay even more than the 40 euros, so for example, a premium of 2%, because this seems to be a good borrower. At a premium of 2%, I could sell this loan for 40.80 euros. This markup would be fair, because I've been running the risk of failure for 6 installments.

On the other hand, it is different if the borrower gets into greater financial difficulties. Here, no investor will be prepared to pay the nominal value of 40 euros, because this indicates a loan default. In this case, it would be necessary to offer a so-called discount. So, for example, 10% to the nominal value. Thus, the offered price would be 36 euros, although the borrower still has to repay 40 euros plus interest.

If all goes well, the buyer has made a good deal. Because he has the full face value again received plus interest and a discount. If the loan fails and the debt collection process can no longer collect anything, there will be a negative return for the buyer.

Simple secondary market without pricing (without surcharges and discounts): Twino

Advanced secondary market with pricing (with surcharges and discounts): Mintos, Bondora

Frequent beginner mistakes

As a buyer, one only pays attention to the indicated return and not to the premium to be paid. Do you pay a higher premium of, for example, 5%, it takes several months until you get to 0 by the interest received first. So you start with such a premium immediately with a negative return. Many investors often forget the scenario of early repayment. Because if a borrower repays early, this can quickly lead to a negative return. Here it is, therefore, recommended not to pay too high surcharges and always include the possibility of early repayment in the calculation. The indicated return is only achieved if the credit runs the entire duration.

20. EXAMPLE PORTFOLIOS

To give you a sense of how such a portfolio can look like on a P2P platform, what the yield differentials between providers can be and what strategies you can follow, let's bring you three examples, based on actual portfolios of investors. Let's start with a very interesting portfolio at the German platform Auxmoney:

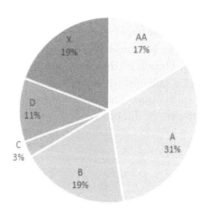

Auxmoney-Portfolio

This portfolio is characterized by a high proportion of almost two-thirds of very secure investments in Auxmoney classes AA, A and B. Probably the return on such a strategy based on Auxmoney would not be very high. However, the portfolio owner has now added the riskiest X-Class loan projects to still drive its yield to a sizeable 8%, and largely skips the Auxmoney scores C and D. This plan can certainly work. All credit requests are manually reviewed and selected by the portfolio owner, which means a high amount of time spent on them, as they do not trust the Portfolio Builder and, therefore, do not use it. Despite the seemingly high risk, he hopes that the manual test will result in a low default rate. Nevertheless, a game with the fire and high personal effort by the high necessary online presence to examine loan offers. To this day, however, the investor was able to hold a return of at least 6%.

Now let's look at the second portfolio, which is based on the featured P2P platform Bondora:

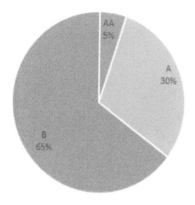

Bondora-Portfolio

In contrast to the first example, this portfolio is very conservative. The owner only invests in loans with the three best Bondora credit ratings AA, A and B, but goes for the supposedly higher risk of investing in a foreign provider. However, this risk is rewarded with a return index of approximately 13%. Furthermore, the time required for the owner of this portfolio is only a few minutes a month, because his loans are fully automatically selected by the Portfolio Builder. He monitors only overdue payments. Although there were some losses over time, the returns remained stable.

In the meantime, you do not even have to choose the credit ratings if you do not want to and you can leave the selection entirely to Bondora's new portfolio builder to make the right investment decisions. Thus, other credit ratings flowed into the portfolio over time and the return even rose to almost 15%. However, the failure rate also increased.

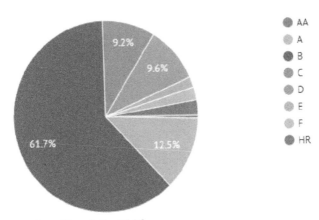

Bondora-Portfolio 2016

The automation of the Bondora portfolio can be set up just as well at Auxmoney to reduce the time to almost zero.

The third portfolio that we will highlight is the one on the popular Mintos buyback platform and based on publicly available data from ourselves that you can track at any time.[62] It differs fundamentally from the portfolios of the Auxmoney and Bondora platforms, as there is no obvious classification by risk class at Mintos.

Mintos operates on a different principle and offers its marketplace for so-called "loan originators" who in turn release loans according to their own security ratings. For example, the company Mogo[63], which offers secured car loans on the platform. These are those that are bought back if the borrower can no longer service the installments. For a complete overview of loan lenders, visit the Mintos website.[64]

Here, too, we fully automatically invest according to certain criteria, according to which we have configured the Portfolio Builder in advance. More than 80% of the current loans are secured by the loan

---

[62] https://passives-einkommen-mit-p2p.de/category/mintos/

[63] http://mogofinance.com/

[64] https://www.mintos.com/en/loan-originators/

originators and cannot be lost as an investment in theory. In the case Mintos or the corresponding loan lender buy back defaulted loans, including the interest incurred until then.

The portfolio we are talking about is running for almost 3 years at the time of writing this book. Some loans were actually repurchased. The return is more than positive.

Mintos-Portfolio of Lars Wrobbel March 2018

As a reminder, the three portfolios described are real portfolios, but are for guidance only and showcase the opportunities in the P2P market. It is not a recommendation for a specific strategy or for one of the three providers used.

21. CORRELATION TO OTHER ASSET CLASSES

In this chapter, we will look at the correlation between P2P loans and other investments. We're pretty sure you'll find this topic as important and valuable to your investments as we do. Because P2P loans have in this matter still a really thick ace up his sleeve.

But before we start, let's take a quick look at what the term "correlation" actually means. A correlation describes (as defined by the official definition[65]) a relationship (interdependence) between two or more features, events, states or functions. The correlation is of considerable importance for investments. The rule is that the smaller the individual investments correlate, the lower the overall risk of the entire portfolio. The ideal diversification is so comprehensive that there are no correlations between the individual asset classes. If you are only in the stock world, this condition is almost impossible. However, as we will soon realize, with a skillful blending of the P2P asset class, it can be a bit closer to this ideal state.

The content of the following graph has been published on the page of the investment tool LendingRobot and shows the correlation of various stock market indices compared to the American P2P market. To understand, you can find below the table of the explanations to the various indices:

---

[65] Further information: https://en.wikipedia.org/wiki/correlation

	VTI	VPACX	VEURX	VBR	VNQ	AGG	TIP	VWEHX	p2p
VTI	**1,00**	0,85	0,88	0,96	0,82	0,08	0,09	0,75	0,19
VPACX	0,85	**1,00**	0,88	0,88	0,69	0,14	0,14	0,67	0,13
VEURX	0,88	0,88	**1,00**	0,82	0,71	0,14	0,15	0,70	0,14
VBR	0,96	0,80	0,82	**1,00**	0,86	0,07	0,07	0,72	0,13
VNQ	0,82	0,69	0,71	0,86	**1,00**	0,26	0,28	0,69	0,18
AGG	0,08	0,14	0,14	0,07	0,26	**1,00**	0,76	0,32	-0,13
TIP	0,09	0,14	0,15	0,07	0,28	0,76	**1,00**	0,33	-0,02
VWEHX	0,75	0,67	0,70	0,72	0,69	0,32	0,33	**1,00**	0,01
p2p	0,19	0,14	0,14	0,13	0,18	-0,13	-0,02	0,01	**1,00**

Correlation to stock market indices [66]

For completeness, here is the breakdown of the abbreviations:
VTI = US Stocks
VPACX = Pacific Stocks
VEURX = European Stocks
VBR = US Small Caps Value
VNQ = US REITs
AGG = US Bonds
TIP = US TIPs
VWEHX = US High Yield Corporate
p2p = P2P-Market

Correlations can take values between -1 and +1. With a value of +1 (or -1), there is a completely positive (or negative) relationship between the characteristics considered. If the correlation coefficient is 0, the two features do not depend on each other at all. As you can see, the P2P asset class does not correlate strongly with any of the listed stock market indices. With the addition of P2P shares to the classic equity portfolio, diversification is thus significantly increased and the correlation between asset classes reduced.

Thus, an admixture of personal loans means additional security for our total assets, which we can and should use. A pure equity portfolio correlates very strongly, which is why an investment in P2P loans can be used as a kind of stabilizer. As a result, the portfolio

---

[66] https://www.lendingrobot.com/

does not suffer from such a strong correlation as would normally be the case and achieves a comparatively better return without the added expense.

Conclusion of this chapter: The P2P market, despite its recent history, is a useful addition to the equity portfolio and you should take advantage of this opportunity, provided you have built up appropriate know-how in this area, understand the investment to be safe on the way of the European P2P-Marketplaces. You're just starting to do that yourself with this book.

22. RISKS AND SAFETY

There are many benefits to investing in P2P loans and most of the European marketplaces we know of are (as we have already seen in our examples) very dedicated to building security and trust, but there are also some risks to consider. This chapter provides you with a detailed explanation of the specific risks and collateral of P2P loans in our view. We have collected these in descending order in a top 5 list for you. We start with the risks:

Risks

1. **Loan defaults:** The biggest and most visible risk to anyone investing in this area is that a borrower cannot repay his loan installments. Most P2P loans are typically not hedged (such as some at Mintos and Auxmoney) with valuables such as real estate, buyback guarantees or residual credit insurance. As we have seen in a diagram in one of the earlier chapters, credit statistics are, for the most part, consumer loans, which in turn can lead to a shortage of missing installments. This conclusion is based on our assumption that people who borrow for consumer goods often lack the necessary financial vision. However, in our experience, most debtors pay on time or with a short delay if they have missed a rate. Nevertheless, you should not neglect the aspect of the credit default and you cannot prevent it, but you can counteract this risk by meaningful diversification. How this works exactly, we have described in the appropriate chapter.

2. **No reliable credit ratings:** Each P2P platform works with companies that check borrowers' creditworthiness in advance, and then scoop each loan request for their probability of

repayment.[67] The lender must be able to rely on the credit rating of the P2P partners, because if they are of poor quality, they can be misleading and make supposedly "safe" credit offers a loss trap. However, anyone who does a good job here and who does a bad job is almost impossible to find out, because each service provider has its own calculation methods in this area, which on the one hand, are secret, and on the other hand, very unlikely to be comparable.

3. **A new financial crisis:** The European P2P market has not yet experienced a real financial crisis (although some of the loan originators of platforms such as Mintos have already lent before the last crisis). We were only able to gather data from the US and, therefore, a rough idea of what could happen.[68] However, how that will affect your personal portfolio is uncertain and depends on many unknown factors. But one thing is certain: for your P2P investment, the financial crisis can be a risk.

4. **Bankruptcy of your P2P platform:** The worst case occurs: The P2P platform you invest in goes bankrupt. Each P2P platform has its own measures and safeguards, so this case does not occur. In the US and also in Europe, many intermediaries use replacement service providers who will continue to operate the platform until the last loans have been repaid. For example, at Auxmoney in Germany, after taking out a loan, the bank takes over everything in the background and, therefore, a similar scenario should apply here as well. In addition, some of the banks are subject to domestic deposit insurance, which will (perhaps) hedge part of the uninvested funds. Here you should inform yourself in advance. However, it remains questionable if

---

[67] Extract from Wikipedia: A credit score is a numerical value based on a statistical analysis that represents the creditworthiness of a person. With credit scoring, companies try to determine the creditworthiness of customers or partner companies more or less automatically according to a given procedure.

[68] https://passives-einkommen-mit-p2p.de/was-passiert-mit-deinem-p2p-portfolio-in-der-finanzkrise/

and how these systems will work when it comes to such cases. Because so far we personally could not gain any experience with such a scenario.

5. **The unpredictable:** The P2P credit market, especially in the Baltics, is still quite young and relatively new in relation to other markets, and it is, therefore, quite possible that cases will occur that nobody has considered in advance. This may be new laws that discriminate against P2P intermediaries, but also any other circumstance that can have side effects on this market. We have no chance to prepare for such things perfectly or to foresee them. However, if you would like to know more about unforeseen events and how to at least arm yourself against them, we recommend the book "The Black Swan" by Nicholas Nassim Taleb (see literature recommendations).

Safeties

1. **Self-responsibility: As described in the chapter** "Diversification", we ourselves can best ensure that our funds are reasonably safe. With various techniques and personal attitudes already described, we can eliminate most of the risks right from the start or at least reduce them. Among other things, it is very important to look at its investor position objectively and not to make decisions from the gut. Remember: this is about your fortune! No path should be too far and no effort too high to protect it.

2. **Credit assessment:** What appears as a risk on the one hand, in our opinion as well as the greatest security? A good and long-term reliable assessment of credit ratings will classify risk offers accordingly in advance. Auxmoney even uses several service providers like Schufa and Arvato Infoscore. An experienced combination that you can rely on to a large extent, as it has been tried and tested for years. All service providers in this field determine their information in our research in two different ways. One variant is the self-search of information and the subsequent provision for their customers (in our case the P2P intermediaries). Many commercial credit bureaus such as

Creditreform, Bürgel, D & B or Coface work this way.[69] The second possible variant is based on the reciprocity principle, which uses the Schufa. Contracting parties of Schufa undertake to pass on certain formalized characteristics to Schufa through the recording and processing of a reportable business. In return, the parties to the contract will receive information from Schufa that other contracting parties have reported to the Schufa about the requested customer.

3. **Deposit guaranty fund (Germany):** As a rule, German intermediaries always have a bank in the background and also handle their business. These banks are usually members of the German Deposit Guarantee Fund. Your funds not already invested in a loan are (probably) safe in the event of a sudden bankruptcy. Abroad, it gets a bit more problematic with this problem, so it is important to check the exact security of the money (if available) before registering on a P2P platform. The money does not necessarily have to be secured, but you should make it clear where your money is and what happens in the event of a platform bankruptcy.

4. **Collection:** Despite high repayment rates in Germany[70] loan default in the banking industry is part of the day-to-day business, and one of the tasks of a P2P broker is to protect investors and mitigate losses. Each collection system works a bit differently, but its essential features are the same. Should any reminders be unsuccessful, the loan will be terminated and the claim will be sold to a collection agency[71]. Collection agencies help creditors get back the money or part of it. So you have to expect discounts here, but this approach saves an investor from a total loss.

---

[69] Creditreform, Bürgel, D&B and Coface are all service provider in the information and risk management.

[70] Over 90% of all privately granted loans are paid on time and over 90% of all persons registered with Schufa have only positive information.

[71] Further information on the functioning of debt collection agencies can be found at https://en.wikipedia.org/wiki/Debt_collection.

However, a debt collection procedure can take months or even years, so the money is initially no longer available after a loan default.

5. **Individual securities:** Individual collateral is not generally available, but more and more providers are seeking to gain a competitive advantage or differentiate themselves from other providers with optional collateral, to emphasize it, and to gain customer confidence. In the Baltics, for example, the buyback guarantee is becoming increasingly popular, and at the editorial deadline, it is already being used by many platforms, including Mintos, Twino, Viventor, Robocash, Viainvest, Swaper and DoFinance. In the case of payment difficulties, the platforms, at first sight, provide the lender with security and protect it from losses. The models are very different and expandable here. We hope that other vendors follow the example of Mintos and Co. and offer collateral as well.

23. BUYBACK GUARANTEE

The repurchase guarantee will reimburse investors for their capital and interest if the borrower does not pay for more than 30 or 60 days. But why? And how do lenders finance the buyback guarantee? Nobody gives away money. Therefore, the money for the repurchased loans must come from somewhere. But where from?

Please note that this chapter reflects and expresses our personal opinion. This chapter is not exhaustive, based on our findings and does not have to correspond to actual circumstances.

It is so beautiful. Simply fantastic. I give my savings to a P2P loan platform, set the auto-investor at a 12% return and enjoy my life. If something happens, the lender jumps in and refunds my losses and even lays the missed interest on top of me because I am such a nice person. Isn't the world beautiful? Do you really believe this?

Have you ever received any money from your bank? Have you ever heard the words from your financial advisor: "Just buy stocks, when they go down, we'll pay you back your money. And we still give you 12% interest on top of that. "Surely you have never heard such a sentence from a bank employee. But why do we hear these statements from the P2P platforms? Why do these platforms offer such protection? Why is my money so important to them? Why do they do that? The answer is short: They do it to make money!

It's always about money! For money and profits. The lenders demand from the borrowers' interest in the three-digit range and in some cases, significantly more. These are not benefactors, they are not Samaritans and they are certainly not worried about your money. Let's take a look at such a lender and how he could work.

How does a lender work?

The loans with a repurchase guarantee offered on the P2P platforms come from so-called "non-bank lenders". As the name implies, these are not banks, but companies which, in the end, individuals like you and me can stand behind. On the Baltic P2P platforms, especially Mintos, the term "loan originator" has established itself.

These "non-bank lenders" lend money. As far as the apparent business model. We try to explain in a somewhat simplified way how that could work in our opinion. If we want to lend 100 euros to a person with our company, then we have to have this 100 euros in advance in our own pocket. That means we need money. The money can come from banks or bonds. For bonds, we do not get the money from the bank, but from investors. A bond has a return, a term and a repayment, just like a normal loan. Only that we are not dependent on the bank but on (risk-taking) investors. In addition to the banks, the lenders can, therefore, come through bonds to their money. So why the P2P platforms at all? Because issuing bonds is complicated, it means work, is subject to laws and investors also want interest rates. There has to be an easier way?

And here our P2P credit platforms come into the game. The platforms offer a more interesting and cheaper way to get new capital. That is our opinion. It must be the cheapest way under the bottom line. The "non-bank lenders" are, like all companies, profit-oriented. If the way through banks or bonds was cheaper, then the P2P platforms would not exist. It is probably not only the cheapest but also the easiest way, in terms of laws and regulations.

What remains is the investor who wants interest. I leave some room for imagination now, claiming that P2P investors could give us more than 12% interest a year, but that interest rates are kept low to finance the buyback guarantee. In our opinion, this could be a way to indirectly allow us, investors, to finance the buyback guarantee.

Because let's be honest, the buyback guarantee has to somehow finance itself. We will not get it for free. So let's ask the next question: Why does the lender buy the loans from us again?

As already stated, the buyback guarantee is, on the one hand, to win the trust of the investors (of us), and on the other hand, it could be through lower interest rates that we co-finance the buyback guarantee itself (at least in part). But the lender is a normal business. Also in the financial industry. And what does every company want?

Right: make money! That's why we are sure there's a third reason why overdue loans are being bought. And that's because it makes money! If, as a P2P investor, one of my many loans fails, I have a problem getting the money. I do not have direct access to this person. For me, the default of a loan is a really big problem.

The lender has completely different cards. This grants thousands of loans. It is part of his daily business that loans are delayed. For this, the lender has a dunning system. And such a dunning system has exactly what? Right: fees! The first reminder in Germany costs about 5 euros, on top. Any further can be more expensive.

If the reminders are also ignored, the lender still has two options:

1. He has his own debt collection department
2. He sells his claims to a collection agency

In both cases, additional fees and lump sums are charged to the borrower. And in both cases, there is still a chance for the lender to get something.

Of course, the dunning process and the collection process cost money, but let's be honest, that's all priced into the original loan. We're talking about interest rates in the triple digits! In order to be able to judge whether or not the buyback guarantee is viable, one would have to know two numbers:

1. In what percentage of the repurchased loans is the dunning process successful?
2. In what percentage was the dunning process unsuccessful, is the collection process successful?

These two numbers would show how healthy and how stable the business is. Unfortunately, P2P platforms and lenders are very taciturn on these issues.

Default rates on Twino, Swaper and Mintos

From Twino we have learned that about 10% of all loans really fail, so where also dunning and debt collection could do nothing more. Swaper has told us that the collection process is tedious and started only in March 2016 and have no concrete figures – but currently, less than 10%. Mintos works with external lenders. Here it is really not easy to get numbers. But Lendo is ~ 2%, Banknote ~ 11.5%, Creamfinance GE ~ 9.5%, Creamfinance DK ~ 1% and Creamfinance CZ ~ 4%.

If the numbers are correct - we cannot control them - then we have a total default rate of between 1% and 11.5%. Assuming the numbers are correct, then the concept could be currently viable. How do we get that? Let's say a lender like Banknote will give you $ 100,000 in credit. For the sake of simplicity, we assume that all loans have a term of 12 months and are at 274.43% interest per annum (interest rate according to Banknote). If we assume Banknote 11% default rate, then 89% of the loans are successful. So 89.000,00 Euro become after 12 months to 332.860,00 Euro. 11% of the loans were canceled completely, there was no single repayment. We have to deduct those 11,000.00 euros from the above income:
332,860.00 euros - 11,000.00 euros makes 321,860.00 euros for Banknote.

Banknote would have made, despite a total loss of 11%, from the 100,000.00 Euro 321,860.00 euros. Sounds like it could work for us. Of course, our bill is a simplistic rough estimate, in which we do not consider costs such as staff, rent, marketing, etc.

If we summarize these considerations, then there is a mathematical calculation behind the buyback guarantee. As long as the balance is not disturbed, the concept is economically viable as long as

- the buyback payments are within reasonable limits.
- the reminder processes and collection processes that start after the buyback have a good success rate.
- the actual interest margins are really high.
- the lender does not get too greedy.

And here's the problem: We as investors cannot judge how this mathematical calculation works. Besides, we cannot control them and we do not even get them when the calculation tilts. The buyback guarantee is simply based on, if you will, promise. How to ensure that this promise can be kept? - Not at all! Every insurance company has to reinsure itself with every promise made by reinsurers. Our buyback guarantee is neither guaranteed nor insured in any way.

Our recommendation

With this presentation, we do not want to vilify the buyback guarantee and certainly not the platforms and the lenders. It works and we benefit from it, every day. But our wish is to make you aware of something. It should now be clear that the buyback guarantee is no guarantee, even if there is the word "guarantee". That's why P2P investments are and remain a high risk and your money could be completely lost.

The exact modalities of how the buyback guarantee is financed are in the dark for us, investors. In addition, the business is not under the eyes of a regulatory authority. Be aware that you know very little about the lenders. How they work, what they have for buffers, what they do for calculations. Even a business report only tells you what was last year, not what it looks like.

The buyback guarantee sounds tempting, no question. But how sure would you feel if the loans did not have a buyback guarantee? Would you invest in these loans if the protection did not exist?

Therefore, our request to you:
- Do not invest too much of your capital in P2P loans!
- Spread your capital across multiple selected platforms!
- Diversify the lenders on every platform!
- Be vigilant and keep trying!

24. TAXATION

Originally this book was published in Germany. The German version, therefore, contains extensive information on domestic taxation. However, you are holding the international version in your hands, so we cannot give you any concrete instructions at this point. It is a fact, however, that distributions from P2P credits, to the best of our knowledge, must be taxed in some way in every country.

If you decide to invest in P2P loans, it is your responsibility to deal with the tax obligations in your home country. There is a lot of learning material on platforms like YouTube. With us in Germany, this investment is also very new for the tax authorities and, therefore, things are constantly changing. So you always have to stay informed in order to be able to take advantage of it in the end.

With German platforms, such as Auxmoney, you will receive a written statement for the tax office once a year, which you can simply attach to your tax declaration. This is usually issued in the first quarter (for Auxmoney, for example, in mid-February). For many non-German platforms, the situation becomes more interesting. Here you are forced to collect your interest income yourself using the research techniques provided. This requires a little effort every year; but once you get the hang of it, it happens pretty quickly; and in our opinion, this effort pays off in any case due to the usually higher returns abroad. Below you can see a simple example of how the P2P platform Mintos filters out the tax-relevant amounts:

Anfangsdatum	Enddatum	Zahlungsart	
01.01.2016	31.01.2016	Zinszahlungen	Auswählen

Heute   Gestern   Diese Woche   Dieser Monat   Letzte Woche   Letzter Monat   Letzter Monat und dieser Monat

Zusammenfassender Auszug

Zinszahlungen

Laden Sie XLSX

Datum	Einzelheiten	Umsatz
05.01.2016	Darlehen Nr. 29694-01 Zinsen	0.09
05.01.2016	Darlehen Nr. 29702-01 Zinsen	0.00
06.01.2016	Darlehen Nr. 29701-01 Zinsen	0.09
11.01.2016	Kredit ID 42956-01 Ruckkauf Zinsen	0.01

Filtering interest for Mintos

However, major platforms such as the above-mentioned P2P platform Mintos and several others are issuing, meanwhile, interest statements and in the next few years the platforms will increasingly adapt to investors.

Tip: For foreign platforms that do not yet offer interest statements, you will usually receive them by e-mail upon request.

In the end, it's not as difficult as it sounds. And once you've done the process for a few years, it'll become a routine that won't be a problem at all.

25. CAN YOU ALSO INVEST WITH YOUR OWN COMPANY?

In short: Yes, you can.

And it does not matter whether it is a corporation or a company constituted under civil law. It is also not necessary to set up your own company specifically for this purpose. I (Kolja) even invest with my own corporation, a Spanish one, in P2P loans and without any problems on 4 different platforms. At Twino, Estateguru, Mintos and Bondora, setting up an account with a company was not a problem at all. Either there is a link directly on the login page to register as a business or a message to the P2P platform support is needed to set up the account. But you need some documents, which I'll point out shortly. At Bondora, I first had a purely private account, so when I wanted to create another account for my company, they built me an elegant combination solution so that I can easily switch back and forth between the accounts.

Unfortunately, I still have not received any feedback from Auxmoney and since I do not maintain a corporate account there, I do not know if this is currently possible.

Reasons for/against a company account on a P2P platform

The reasons for a corporate account can be manifold, for me, it was/is the fact that all money, which is distributed from a company to a partner or managing director, is subject to income tax. In terms of corporate governance, it is, therefore, worth considering investing company money in P2P loans or other investments. Of course, interest earned by a company must be taxed just as much as by a private individual, but if there is simply more capital available in the business than one owns as a private individual, then it may make sense. In addition, I consider it a useful diversification, especially when you think about that many smaller companies have a large lump risk, if they operate only in a niche or are dependent on a few customers.

Imagine, you run a craft business with five employees and are 80% dependent on two large companies that bring you the bulk of your sales. If an order should be dropped, a company can quickly get into liquidity shortages. Of course, investing in your own company is always the priority, so I only use real free cash flows to invest in stocks or P2P loans, which I DO NOT need for investment in the operational business and its growth.

Especially with new offerings, such as the Bondora Go & Grow feature, there is a good opportunity here to intervene between retained earnings, even if it is only 4-5 months. Then you pay taxes on an interest income, but in the meantime, you can sometimes earn some money from 5,000 or 10,000 euros, which you do not need in the company (with the corresponding risk, of course).

Also, consider the following: A limited liability company (sole proprietorship anyway) may be liable for all assets of the company in doubt, including debt, equity, etc. In other words, the company's investments are not suddenly swift in the event of (imminent) bankruptcy transferable into private property, but serve creditors of the company in doubt as a bankrupt estate. So every entrepreneur will always seek a balance between private wealth and business assets and not be too "poor" in the private sector just to potentially save a few taxes. Or at least the investments over a certain size even spread over several enterprises.

Furthermore, I would not set up a business just to invest in P2P loans unless the sums invested are actually on the order of magnitude justifying the (financial) effort needed to run a business. With costs for tax consultants, accounting, etc. of several hundred to even a thousand euros a year, that can make the P2P return maggoty. I prefer a classic step-by-step approach to such matters.

Requirements for a company account

If you decide to set up a corporate account with one or more P2P platforms, you're probably wondering what you need it for. First of all, you need a copy of the company's deed of incorporation, which has been notarized. In addition, the platforms will need a copy of your ID card or ID card from other managing or authorized partners or persons of the company.

Furthermore (although this varies from one platform to another), it may be that you are requesting a copy of the commercial register. If you already own a company but do not have an extract, you can apply for it at any time.

The costs of this amount to about 10-50 € (it depends on your country), where it makes sense to apply for a notarized certificate and extract, as you also for many other services needed.

An LEI number (Legal Entity Identifier), which is mandatory for all companies from 2018 to settle securities transactions, is not required to register with a company with a P2P provider (as of August 2018).

26. THE 10 BIG MISTAKES IN P2P INVESTMENTS

To avoid mistakes, you first have to know them. For this purpose, we have inserted this chapter. After thoroughly reading and internalizing the individual points, you should be able to identify your mistakes as quickly as possible and use tactics to avoid them.

1. **Lack of diversification:** As mentioned in the introduction, you should stick to the principle "Do not put all the eggs in one basket" not only in your entire portfolio but also in the individual asset classes. Because if this one basket falls to the ground, a large part of your eggs is no longer usable. This applies analogously to the P2P investment also to your portfolio. Unfortunately, as a lender, we cannot influence the repayment morale of borrowers unless we call him and threaten him with a baseball bat. However, we should better leave that to debt collection companies specializing in debt collection.

    So we have to come to terms with the idea that some loans will turn out well or bad over time. Depending on the platform and the scoring of the respective borrower, the default rate varies considerably but is generally no higher than for normal banks. The risk is, therefore, statistically not greater, just because it is a P2P investment.

    However, if you have invested your entire capital in a loan and just this fails, the entire capital is lost. No matter how good the credit rating is. For this reason, you should spread your investment amount to several loans. How this spread is built-in, you have to decide based on the size of your personal portfolio. You've already come to know strategies for successful diversification. Now it is important to apply them successfully and, above all, in the long term.

2. **Start immediately with large sums:** Many people want immediate results when it comes to investing. This sometimes

causes you to act headless and start with too much. Especially if you only start with one or two platforms at the beginning, this behavior can be fatal.

So start with very small sums and save yourself an oversized pudding. This rule also applies to the investment in individual loans. Do not overdo it here and remember point number 1. This, combined with a relatively small amount of funding, can be enough to make your first investment on a P2P platform really fun. It also makes you feel safer with time.

3. **Lack of trust:** "Uncertainty" is the biggest enemy in this third mistake. In many forum contributions, one finds "damaged" investors who "report" on their bad experiences with P2P or other investments. But this mainly results from the fact that people in forums report mainly on their bad experiences, less on the good ones. A phenomenon that can be found in almost every area of life.

Take this book as an example. If you find it bad, you may be annoyed with the money you spend and write us a bad review on Amazon. But will you also write us a good review if you like the book? We would like to, but we are aware that only very few readers will do so. Another example that every worker will know: the supervisor sees the bad things rather than the good ones. You can perform well all year round, but if you notice negatively before the end of the year, your boss will remember it rather than your good performance.

The same is true in P2P and other investments. In our opinion, the calculation implies that more than 2% of an asset class could get a return on investment without even taking any significant risk. You just have to make it clear that you are not bringing any money to the bank on a fixed-rate savings account, which is secured by the government. You know that: In the past, negative news frequently dominated the press landscape in terms of general investment outside of savings accounts or insurance:

"Prokon insolvent, thousands of investors broke"
"Conergy files insolvency petition, future of investor capital uncertain"

The scenery of the examples is expandable and fills several books. Warren Buffett once said that you should not invest unless you are willing to take risks, and so does the P2P investment. If you lose your nerve at the first loan default, you better start looking for other alternatives for your investments. That's fine.

4. **Investing despite the lack of experience:** It's always terrifying how many investors blindly invest their hard-earned money somewhere without just reading a book (like this one). You hear without your own research on friends, colleagues or worse: acquaintances and consultants; all because you are not willing to take a book in your own hands or to inform yourself otherwise.

This is not only a high risk but also gives off even its financial responsibility, by simply making someone responsible for a lossy investment, because the idea (so to speak) did not come from oneself. One had no time, had to work, learn, watering flowers or find any other excuse to give up his financial responsibility.[72] One invests 20,000 - 30,000 euros from an inheritance without first researching exactly what actually happens with the money and whether not about 10% of the sum immediately in the pockets of a consultant or elsewhere wander.

On the other hand, the next supermarket weekly is regularly and accurately studied for discounts in the cent area. It does not cost more than 30 minutes and 5 - 20 Euro, to find now on every topic at least a good book or even free webinars on the internet. This invested time and the little money are often worth pure gold. Because knowledge helps to effectively save costs, to get more security and thus to build responsibility in dealing with their own finances. Ultimately, this leads to an increase in the return. So that you get suggestions, we have put together a few

---

[72] This is also called "passive life". Failure to do so can blame other people, rather than admitting to themselves, having failed to find suitable measures or experience, to be successful or to reconsider their actions in case of failure.

literature recommendations for you at the end of this book.

5. **Constant change of p2p platforms:** Just like in the stock market, the motto is "back and forth makes pockets empty," because any type of investment ultimately costs money in the form of fees or time. The platforms want and should, of course, also make money, otherwise, they would not exist and we would have no opportunity to invest on the internet. Now there is a competition with P2P platforms as well as with banks, bakers, automakers etc. The more investor money a platform collects, the more credits it can lend and the faster the credit balance for the claimant is confirmed. So it is in the nature of things that P2P providers want to make their offer as attractive as possible, both to borrowers and to investors.

For this reason, one will always see interesting "exchange offers" in comparisons, whereby the change here, of course, cannot be equated with a change of equity portfolios. These are (more) classic advertising offers, such as temporary fee waivers, bonus credits or cashbacks, to win you over as a new investor. The "switching costs" also refer more to the individuality of the various P2P providers. Each platform has different conditions and special features and you have to gain experience first, you spend a lot of time and almost always pay according to training. This is almost inevitable when changing. We, therefore, recommend that you first select a platform and gain experience there. Which one you choose is up to you. You should have received enough guidance and suggestions for the correct selection of a proper provider in this book.

Another trap that we often observe in this context is the change of provider due to a lack of credit availability. It sometimes happens that a platform has a bottleneck in the credit supply. Especially the smaller ones often do that. The consequence for many investors is to deduct money and place somewhere else. Here we can say from our experience that this reaction is overdone, because the credit supply usually improves automatically after a few weeks and sometimes months. We have never had the case that our money was not invested for this reason.

6. **To spend too much time on credit selection:** The most important asset of an investor is not his money but his time. This is a lesson we usually only understand when our time in life is limited by factors such as family, job or the like. For us, in addition to the ROI[73] the most important key figure is, therefore, ROTI[74]. In short, this means that we would rather settle for a 5% return and work effectively for only 20 minutes a day, rather than 7%, but spend 6 hours a day.

   On the other hand, we can use the "time capital" that we save through this compromise to improve the investment (through books, training, etc.) and ourselves. The result could be based on our example: After improving our skills by the time saved, we can still achieve the 7% return with 20 minutes a day or maybe more. However, if we continue to invest a lot of time in credit selection, we will not have a chance to learn new things at all. When it comes to investing in personal loans, we should look for providers who have automatic portfolio builders on offer. Because only with this we have the possibility of maximum time savings. What these automated portfolio builders are doing and how they work, you have already learned and hopefully remember. Otherwise, look again in the appropriate chapter. Even if they seem a bit complicated at first and do not invest perfectly right away, it pays to stay tuned and use the tools provided.

7. **Emotional choices:** Being involved with "feeling" may make sense when you have a date with a pretty woman, but not when investing in personal loans or any other asset class. Feelings lead us to short-circuit reactions, which can have fatal consequences

---

[73] Return on Investment: The term "return on investment" (ROI for short, also: return on capital, return on investment, return on capital, return on assets) is a business measure for measuring the return on an entrepreneurial activity, measured in terms of profit in relation to capital employed (Entry from Wikipedia).

[74] Return on time invested: The term "return on time invested" is a measure of the ultimate return on an investment

for our finances. So we should not only see our investment in the P2P market as a long-term investment, but we should try to handle it as well. This means that we need to come to look at our portfolio only once a month or perhaps even less frequently. What seems unthinkable is made possible by the tools offered by the portfolio builder. Gerald Hörhan[75] often speaks of the "perfectly scalable and emotionless investment system" and that should be our ultimate goal in every asset class. Switch off emotions through automatic investing, keep your feet still and adjust and configure as needed. We know that this is not an easier path and it takes time, but in our opinion, it is the best way to go.

8. **Wrong Investment Strategy:** Many newcomers to the P2P investment are unaware that their money will be tied up for years if you do not pay attention to the repayment term. 5 years look at 25 euros, after no particularly long binding and the seductive "bid-button" in addition to the high yield number lures. But once the money is in the pot, it's gone and it's still uncertain whether you'll ever see it again.

From the beginning, you should think about how long term you want to invest and whether you might need the money at short notice. This you can then control over short-term loans. The lowest maturity is 12 months for most providers. However, shorter runtimes are also possible (for example with Twino). There is a kind of "ejection seat" on all P2P platforms with a secondary market. Here you can quickly sell your investments (usually at a discount) and the money goes back to your account. But all these possibilities and contingencies have to be considered before starting an investment, and maybe even **before** choosing a provider.

9. **Ignoring Costs:** Those who ignore the cost of long-term transactions or similar tend to be much worse off (and we're not

---

[75] Excerpt from Wikipedia: Gerald Hörhan is an Austrian manager, investor and author. He is best known for his controversial wealth planning and criticisms of the European Union.

talking about peanut amounts) than someone who does 5 minutes of research to find a cheap provider. The cost structure of P2P platforms is not uniform, but highly individual and is also constantly changing. The following table shows the costs of some platforms at the time of writing this book:

P2P platform	Primary market	Secondary market
Auxmoney.com	1%	–
Bondora.com	0%	0%
Lendico.com	1%	–
Zencap.com	1%	–
Ablrate.com	0%	0%
Investly.eu	0%	–
Estateguru.com	0%	–
SavingStream.co	0%	0%
Mintos.com	0%	0%
Crosslend.de	1%	–
Twino.eu	0%	0%

Fees of P2P platforms

It should be noted here that the percentages often refer to different calculation bases. More detailed information about the fees can be found on the pages of the respective P2P platforms.

You can see at first glance that with a large number of providers, you can dodge those who have costs. Provided the paid provider does not have any value-added features that could justify a selection, such as a very comfortable portfolio builder. So compare regularly the costs of your favorite providers to see if another investment would be worthwhile to another provider or maybe it would be rewarding to move your current portfolio there. According to our observation, and as you can easily see in the chart, the trend is strong in giving the investor any fees.

10. **Want to reach fast wealth through P2P:** P2P is not a free ticket for fast wealth. Even though you may see and achieve dream returns of 20% and sometimes even more with some providers, you should always be aware that return comes from risk and these two values correlate strongly positively. If the

return is high, the risk is generally high. As an example you can see a screenshot of the expected returns from the provider Crosslend, ranked by rating and risk class:

Risikoklasse	Prognostizierte Erträge
A	0,22% - 3,47%
B	2,99% - 5,06%
C	4,01% - 6,25%
D	4,68% - 8,32%
E	5,27% - 11,37%
F	5,81% - 12,88%
G	6,65% - 14,03%
HR	> 13,45%

Expected return

Do not blind your eyes to the expected effective rate of interest and do not transfer your monthly salary to the accounts of the lowest-rated borrowers. You should approach the investment seriously and professionally. Build your portfolio slowly, gain experience and ultimately get the return that fits your personal risk profile. The write-off rate can be very high and you have to be able to absorb it first if half of the portfolio consists of payments that are long overdue and about to be collected.

27. P2P LENDING & FINANCIAL FREEDOM
written by Tobias Lindner from p2p-lending-at-its-best.com

Do you still remember the friends book, you received in school? Where are you from? What is your favorite food? Whom is your best friend? And a lot of other questions about your life. But there was the one question, which I hated: What do you want to become later in your life? My answer: Living from my financial assets by the age of 45.

To be honest, I forgot about this goal. I went to school and studied later at university. Quite "normal" and, of course, I entered a job beside my university time. Two job changes and three kids later I was reminded of my goal about two years ago. I thought about my goals in life, when this idea came back to my mind.

Today you would probably say: "Becoming financially independent through passive income". A lot of buzzwords. But it hits the sense of the friends book. But how to get there? I am now aged 38, so it is another 6.5 years to go until the age of 45.

In the past two years, I read constantly books from people, who made it financially. And everything they did was just a bit more, than the average. I mean, just check the statistics. About 2.5 hours per day we are busy with our smartphone. Another 3-4 hours we are watching television. There is plenty of time to beat the average.

Setting up my financial income streams

Everyone out of my books, videos and courses started with a plan – something I did not have in life until then. In 2016 I wrote my first books with Lars and started my new side business career. After several months the first Euros arrived at my account and I started to invest. At first, it was just in ETFs like Kolja and several more suggested it.

And this is how I came to P2P lending. I mean, you are not able to walk further on in your life recognizing, that P2P loans are paying you 10-15% of interest rate. Maybe you could, but I was not able to. Therefore, I invested my first money into P2P in 2016. At first, I was investing manually. Every Friday evening, I was sitting at home with a big glass of wine, choosing good P2P loans at Mintos and Bondora. When it got to a bottle of wine I changed to the auto-invest.

How to maximize your interest rate!

Getting financially independent requires quite a lot of money in my case. The level of security is probably a bit higher with kids, so I am still in my fulltime job. But I have goals and this is where my job is able to help me. I am doing everything besides my job in the evening hours, so any additional income is for my investments.

If I want to replace my today's salary through passive income, I probably need more than a million Euros. So, I tried quite a lot of the "get-rich-fast"-things, but nothing worked. But P2P lending still pays me 10-15%, so why not try it!? I calculated for my self and found out, that I am quite risky with my asset allocation. Not really wondering about it, because my fulltime-income is still there. All my needs and expenses are secured for the moment, that I am able to invest a bit riskier.

I am investing in shares, dividend shares and ETFs as well, but I decided to invest about 30% into P2P lending. Why not use that interest rate booster for my financial independence? In my eyes, there is no serious possibility to get more interest rate without investing more money or more time. Of course, there are possibilities like, for example, day trading, but I do not have the time, therefore, and I am not willing to invest this time. I tried and failed, because I have not understood it.

Set up your own asset allocation

I learned a lot about financial things in the last years. But this knowledge is nothing without taking action. I took some time to understand, that for me, it is not the right decision to hunt for a higher interest rate. The right thing for me is to work on my income becoming bigger and bigger.

P2P lending is the part I have lots of fun with. Investing in ETFs or dividend shares is fun as well, but the interest rate is "just" about 3-8%. No word, that is quite a lot more than on your day money account. But investing in P2P lending and getting interest payments every day is somehow more motivating.

And meanwhile, you are able to diversify your P2P portfolio as well. There are quite a lot of platforms offering you P2P loans from all over the world. So, can even diversify a bit of the risk away through diversification your P2P platforms and loans.

Financial freedom through P2P lending?

Kolja is calculating with a very interesting indicator: ROTI! This indicator is an own-developed calculation for "Return On Time Invested". As I am not working in a bank and I do not have six or seven figures in my account, it is essentially for me, how much money I am able to earn. Just imagine EUR 10k in your account. What is the outcome of a lot of time-investment to higher your interest rate from 15% to 20%? Right, it is 500 Euros.

But let's say you have to invest 50 hours to reach these 5% more of your interest rate. What is your hour-rate? Exactly, it is 10 Euros. As I am not a financial guru I think I need to invest about 50 hours. And beside this time invested the risk will rise as well as.

I think investing my time into actions is more useful, which raise my income. There are a lot of digital jobs you can work on and earn more than 10 Euros per hours. But this is just the one hand. On the other hand, your personal interest income will raise, when you invest this money.

Let's just say you earn 10 Euros per hour but invest the money after receipt. Your interest rate will still be 15%, but 15% on 10,5k this month, 11k next month...and so on. Within one year you will reach 16k, without any more risk. For me, the growth of my abilities and knowledge always beats the higher interest which you can get for more risk.

P2P lending is a good opportunity

Everyone recognizes P2P lending is affected by the high interest rate. Not wondering about that, but also P2P lending is quite risky. Please do never invest everything of your money into P2P loans. Check your asset allocation and if you are interested you can diversify your P2P portfolio as well. But P2P lending should be always just a part of your whole asset portfolio.

On my blog, you will find my current investments. Besides my personal opinion, there are also some hard facts. I am not able to give you any advice about your investment. I am just showing you on my blog which way I take and how it works out. There are several investment models. I rely on those from people, who are successful with those models in the long run.

Gerd Kommer is a German investment banker who showed, that intelligent and diversified investing minimizes your risk. And additionally, this way of investing can be automated. You have to decide once what is right for you. After setting all up, you can focus on your income streams again. That is quite my style, like I want to invest and live.

As Kommer just focused on the stock market, P2P lending is, of course, not included in his model. But I took the model and changed it. Instead of bonds, I choose to take P2P lending. And I also worked on the weighting of the shares of my portfolio.

Now my portfolio is damn simple and automated. It is just an hour per month I have to invest in my portfolio and do some transactions. That is it and I can fully focus on my income-producing-actions, as I call them.

Reaching financial freedom in 2025

I do not know yet, what "financial freedom" is for me. Until now, I define it as income, which pays my expenses. I do not want to stop working. It is just reaching the freedom to do what I want. Therefore, I do not think that it has to be millions, which are on my account. I would also take them, of course.

But money is not everything. For me, it is something to fulfill my dreams and goals in life. When my savings and side business incomes will be enough to pay my salary from my job today, I will feel like financially independent.

So, whatever your goal is, maybe you do not have to hunt for the highest interest rate or the latest possibility. P2P lending, as well as ETFs investing or dividend shares, are mainly without cost or just little fees. Focus on getting your income streams bigger than on the next 5% of the interest rate. With P2P lending you get 10-15% of the interest. ETFs and dividend shares have about 8-12% per year (8% average growth plus a dividend of 3-4%). Your money will double every 6-7 years.

Earning and investing of about EUR 30k per year as an example will give you assets of about EUR 340k in seven years. 10% of this sum is EUR 34k per year and EUR 2,5k per month. Is this financial freedom to you? For me, it is the right way to get there.

28. STUDIES AND TESTS

"Yes, but is that safe? What if my money is gone?"

In addition to the risks of P2P lending mentioned in this book, there is, of course, the point to mention that while platforms such as the ones presented in this book perform credit checks, the quality of these tests to this day is very non-transparent to investors. Seals and stamps are created quickly and, therefore, it is, of course, interesting for you as a reader and also for us as authors to know what independent institutions have to say. After our intensive research, this results in a mixed picture.

In the United States, where debts are more commonplace than in other countries, credit default rates of up to 20% were partially reached by 2008. That has changed, however, since the SEC[76] has rigorously intervened in the US and made the rules of the game stricter. According to US scientist Robert B. Lamb of the Leonard N. Stern School of Business in New York, P2P lending is a "solid business", which can be seen in the fact that the industry has up to three-digit growth rates annually, and that would hardly be possible if a large number of loans could not be serviced and thousands of investors would go home without a return.

As the P2P market in other countries is still in its infancy, the reviews and statements of independent institutions are also scarcer. The "Stiftung Warentest" in Germany has two reports about the provider Auxmoney and Smava, once taken to the chest and comes to an overall positive conclusion. While 2010[77] was still criticized for "misleading advertising" and "long confirmation times for borrowers", which led to borrowers being asked to pay even if they

---

[76] The United States Securities and Exchange Commission (SEC) is the US Securities and Exchange Commission for the supervision of securities trading in the United States.

[77] https://www.test.de/Privatkredite-ueber-Auxmoney.com-Falle-fuer-Kreditsuchende-4146282-0/

did not get a loan, 2013[78] report sounded more positive: "Both providers (Auxmoney and Smava) are today an alternative to banks for loan seekers. For people whose credit rating is not the best, the loan can be even cheaper than at the bank. Risk-averse lenders can generate good returns."

In 2014, the largest study ever on P2P in Europe was conducted by the University of Cambridge[79]. Among other things, it analyzed the growth rates of different "alternative" financing methods in Europe. The study's findings suggest that the alternative financing sector, to which P2P lending contributes most, is gaining more importance in Europe, though with some differences between countries. For example, England was the largest growth driver, accounting for more than 80% of the lending volume in alternative financing in 2015. Overall, the university estimated that the transaction volume of alternative online funding methods will amount to 7 billion euros.

It was criticized that countries such as Italy made poor access to alternative financing possible, which could, for example, have a negative impact on macroeconomic development due to heavy regulation.

The following statistics should clarify the importance and the growth of alternative financing models:

---

[78] https://www.test.de/Smava.com-und-Auxmoney.com-Privatkredite-im-Internet-4540421-4540426/

[79] The entire study can be downloaded from:
http://www.jbs.cam.ac.uk/fileadmin/user_upload/research/centres/alternative-finance/downloads/2015-uk-alternative-finance-benchmarking-report.pdf

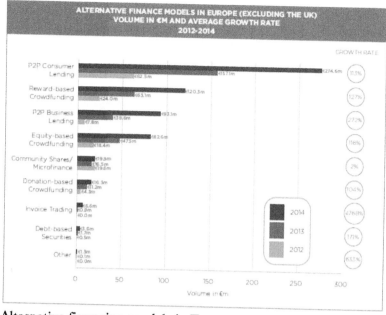

Alternative financing models in Europe

This statistic shows the market volume of alternative online financial services in Europe excluding the UK from 2012 to 2014, broken down by funding type. These alternative forms of financing include financial channels and financial instruments that arise outside traditional finance. Examples of these alternative channels are online platforms for equity-based crowdfunding[80] or today's form of peer-to-peer lending. Alternative financing instruments include SME mini-bonds[81], private placements[82], as well as other mechanisms of the so-called "shadow banking system"[83], social impact bonds[84] and

---

[80] Equity-based "swarm financing"

[81] Bond subscription of small medium-sized companies to finance investments.

[82] Private, non-public sale (placement) of assets.

[83] For example, subsidiaries of banks that operate outside bank balance sheets or companies that engage in financial activities within the legal framework but are not themselves credit institutions, such as hedge funds or private equity funds.

[84] A policy and funding instrument that privately finances social services and, if successful, publicly reimburses them.

alternative currencies such as Bitcoin[85]. In 2012, the German online market for alternative forms of financing in the area of P2P consumer lending reached a volume of around 20 million euros. In 2015, the volume was already well over 100 million euros, and the trend is rising.[86]

Meanwhile, there is an expanded study by the University of Cambridge titled "Sustaining Momentum",[87] which has confirmed the growth trend of the first study. It is based on data from 367 crowdfunding, P2P credit and various other providers of alternative financing models from 32 European countries. The result of this study is that the European market outside the UK has increased by 72%. Here are the results in detail:

---

[85] English for "binary digit coin", is a worldwide decentralized payment system and the name of a digital monetary unit. Further information can be found at https://en.wikipedia.org/wiki/Bitcoin
[86] More can be found at:
https://de.statista.com/statistik/daten/studie/408548/umfrage/markt volumen-online-finanzdienste-in-deutschland- nach-finanzierungsform/
[87] More about the study at https://www.jbs.cam.ac.uk/faculty-research/centres/alternative-finance/publications/sustaining-momentum

Financing model	Market volume of 2015
Peer-to-Peer Consumer Lending	365.000.000 Euro
Peer-to-Peer Business Lending	212.000.000 Euro
Equity-based Crowdfunding	159.320.000 Euro
Reward-based Crowdfunding	139.270.000 Euro
Invoice Trading	80.590.000 Euro
Real Estate Crowdfunding	26.970.000 Euro
Donation-based Crowdfunding	21.710.000 Euro
Debt-based Securities	10.730.000 Euro
Balance Sheet Business Lending	2.350.000 Euro
Profit Sharing Crowdfunding	540.000 Euro

Excerpt from "Sustaining Momentum" - volumes by segment in Europe 2015 (excluding the UK)

It will be interesting to see if the growth rates of personal loans will persist.

At the end of 2016, there was also a study by the German Bundesbank to investigate how P2P lending fits into the credit market, focusing in particular on the following questions:

Why do private households use P2P platforms as financial intermediaries? Are interest rates on P2P loans in Germany higher than those of banks? Are P2P loans riskier than bank loans? Is Internet-based P2P lending complementary or substitutive to bank lending?

The results show that loans from P2P platforms earn more interest than loans made through the banking system and that they are riskier. However, when the underlying risk differentials are adjusted, interest rates are comparable. In addition, the analysis shows that lending through P2P platforms correlates negatively with banks. The results also show that for high-risk borrowers, bank lending is being replaced in favor of P2P lending, as banks are unwilling or unable to serve this market segment.[88]

---

[88] The study for download: http://www.p2p-kredite.com/deutsche-bundesbank-privatkredite.pdf

Personally, we find the relatively rapid development or "take-over" of alternative financing ideas in each country remarkable. A historical example: The first exchange-traded fund[89] (ETF) was introduced in America back in the 1970s (even though they had a different name at that time). But it took decades before these investment products were "discovered" even in Europe. This was much faster with P2P lending, as providers were able to copy things that worked in a shorter time thanks to the Internet. However, it may well be that in a few years a few large P2P platforms will have become established and take over the business of smaller intermediaries, which then either completely disappear from the market or are bought up by the large platforms.

In addition, it should also be said that platforms from abroad in the official German tests remain completely unnoticed, but in our personal opinion, they are in many parts ahead by a nose. However, there are now a number of personal reports from private investors on the Internet (including us), which in many cases speak a very clear and above all positive language. You can find many of these reviews on the linked websites at the end of this book.

---

[89] An exchange-traded fund (ETF) is an investment fund that is traded on a stock exchange.

29. STUDY RESULTS IN DETAIL

The area around Asia and the Pacific was in 2016 with 221 billion euros, the world's largest market for alternative financing. By contrast, the American continent, with a market volume of around 32 billion euros, looks small in comparison. However, we must not forget the European market, including the market leader Great Britain, because, in fact, the European market was the smallest of this group with around 7 billion euros. The Chinese market claimed an unbelievable 99% of the volume in the Asia-Pacific region but still put in 134% annual growth. In this context, China is already the future and in the coming years, we will have to look more and more about our European counterparts in order not to be left behind. This as a comment, because more than 75% of the replies of the following study came from European platforms.

Important with all numbers on this and the following pages is to enjoy them with care. Although the Expanding Horizons[90] report, which we will refer to below, was written by outstanding Cambridge University scientists, the numbers are just an indicator. A total of 344 crowdfunding and P2P platforms, as well as other intermediary financial intermediaries from 45 countries, were surveyed and these results compiled. We will now cut down the 120 pages to a few and try to give you the most value from this study.

The development in the industry this year can actually be summed up in a few words. The main driver is the increasing professionalization. The acceptance of P2P among institutional investors is also associated with this. Institutional investors are pension funds, investment funds, asset managers and banks. In the

---

[90] Ziegler, T., Shneor, R., Garvey, K., & Wenzlaff, K. (2018). *Expanding Horizons - The Third European Alternative Finance Report*. Cambridge, United Kingdom: University of Cambridge. Online under:
https://www.jbs.cam.ac.uk/fileadmin/user_upload/research/centres/alternative-finance/downloads/2018-02-ccaf-exp-horizons.pdf

area of P2P consumer loans, institutional investors already financed 45% of total lending volume in 2016, compared with 26% of the previous year's volume. These investors were particularly strong in Spain, Italy and the Baltic States. A platform like Mintos, which among other things specializes in consumer loans and has invested 500 million euros in investments in February 2019, will thus be supported to a large extent by these investors. In the area of P2P real estate financing, institutional investors accounted for 46% of the volume in 2016.

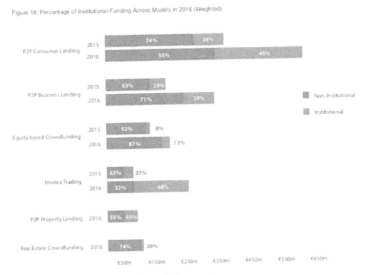

Figure 18: Percentage of Institutional Funding Across Models in 2016 (Weighted)

Development of institutional financing

Whether this development is good or bad, everyone has to decide for themselves. In our opinion, the biggest advantage of "institutionalizing P2P" is the security gained for private investors, because if this were not the case, we would seriously wonder if this business model has a real future.

For us, the money of these professional investors is the guarantor of a future-oriented asset class, because this group of investors employs many well-paid experts who invest their investment volume only in promising projects. A bad or long-term unprofitable project may perhaps be supported in the short term by private investors, as they believe in the project. But professional investors will have created numerous models and invest only after careful consideration and many meetings. An increase of 26% to 45% on this scale represents, for us, a confirmation of the exposure to personal loans and gives us more confidence as a private investor in this rather risky investment area.

It is also to be expected that institutional investors will not deduct their money from one day to the next. So when it comes to the next flattening of the economy or even an economic crisis that is a recurring process in our world, it is likely to be those investors who are only likely to subtract their money. In our opinion, it will also be these investors who will be the "rock in the surf" for P2P. This is because retail investors buy too many financial products, then sell them back to their lowest price at the low point of the next crisis, as the fear of further loss plays such a big role here. Institutional investors will probably keep a cool head in a future crisis and perhaps invest less new funds in the somewhat riskier personal loan business, but we do not expect a kind of "sell off" of loans at junk prices.

Another trend that has been contributing to the professionalization and growing of the industry for years is the increasing use of automated portfolio builders, which are already covered in a chapter in this book. The simplicity of use is undisputed and many users will certainly make their lives easier as their investment preferences are unlikely to change over a few days or weeks. One should not change the fund in the savings plan every month. Ultimately, one would only get a confusing collection.

Once you have made a decision, you should stay with it. This also applies to personal loans. However, there may always be changes in the market. For this reason, it makes sense to look regularly into the investor account, to possibly add loan lenders from new countries explicitly to their own auto-invest and thereby, for example, to obtain greater diversification. However, it is also possible to exclude certain loan lenders if the information available on the loan lender is insufficient or if one does not want to invest in a particular country.

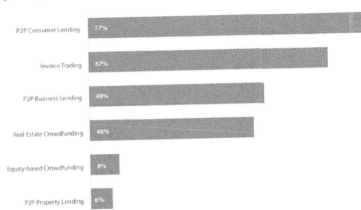

Figure 19: Proportion of Auto-Selection by Models 2016

Abbildung 41: Where are portfolio builders used?

There are two major benefits to the intermediary platforms. On the one hand, users are becoming more and more tied to the respective platform, as the proceeds from the loans do not flow into the investor's account or even bank account but remain on the platform and are invested in new loans, as the investor imagines. This creates predictable liquidity for the platform. In addition to this point, on the other hand, the loan lenders are more tied to the platform, as they can better plan their future lending. Without this function, there would be hardly any credit in one month, and in the next, all investors would invest double the usual amount. This would result in a troubled market and probably also growing displeasure, as investors' money is not continually being reinvested, and because of this short term "parking" the money cannot generate returns for the investor. When, a few years ago, P2P was still far less developed, interest and principal actually flowed into the bank account. Today, the whole thing is almost unimaginable.

At that time, we always checked our accounts balance at the end of the month to see if our funded projects had paid their installments on time. Also, there was a minimum investment of 25 € on many platforms. And we invested a lot in a project that turned out to be a particularly bad decision.

In our opinion, the portfolio builder, therefore, is the most important interface between investor and platform. But as a beginner, you should not lose sight of the diversification, just because you have invested in many loan projects. Diversification through loan lenders and countries in auto-invest is just as important.

High use of this function means that the functions in Auto-Invest are becoming ever more numerous and detailed - a big plus for us as a private investor. Who does not like to control in detail what should happen to his money and then simply leans back?

For those who really want to know, platforms like Bondora today even offer the option of investing via the API interface. This allows anyone who wants to set their own criteria and is not satisfied with the pre-selection of criteria in Auto-Invest to set their own parameters for investing. However, knowledge of programming is necessary. But in our opinion, an extended auto-investment is enough.

Here, we definitely see a trend towards improving auto-invest and expect other major platforms to create API interfaces alongside Bondora. The effect of professionalization with its institutional investors is also likely to contribute to this, as these professionals want to control even more precisely where their money goes.

Apart from these obvious innovations, the platforms we invest in are mostly companies that have been on the market for less than ten years. Maybe that's why the focus of these companies is on new products. Released by Bondora, Go & Grow offers investors the opportunity to earn 6.75% in annual returns, while liquidating the account at any time without discount. In the field of consumer credit, around 59% of the active platforms in 2016 announced that they had significantly adjusted their products.

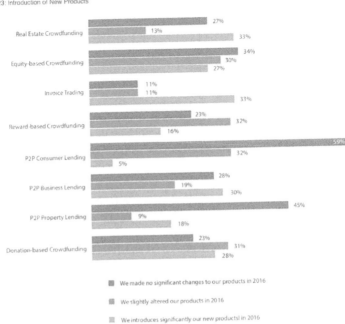

Figure 23: Introduction of New Products

Real Estate Crowdfunding 27% / 13% / 33%

Equity-based Crowdfunding 34% / 30% / 27%

Invoice Trading 11% / 11% / 33%

Reward-based Crowdfunding 23% / 32% / 16%

P2P Consumer Lending 59% / 32% / 5%

P2P Business Lending 28% / 19% / 30%

P2P Property Lending 45% / 9% / 18%

Donation-based Crowdfunding 23% / 31% / 28%

▨ We made no significant changes to our products in 2016

▨ We slightly altered our products in 2016

▨ We introduces significantly our new productsl in 2016

Introduction of new products

P2P will not be an industry that lingers at a standstill. We can look forward to further innovations and a young company could revolutionize the market with an innovative solution. If you do something, you should do it right. So it's important to always stay up to date, because a new product could fit even better to your own investment style than the old one.

But not only are the visible processes important. Combining new financial products and leveraging automated portfolio builders makes it more important than ever to have working structures behind the scenes. With Auto-Invest we give the platforms a big advance in confidence. A sufficient capital base of the companies, a well-functioning selection process of the borrowers and a correct evaluation of the credit risks must be guaranteed thereby. Here, platforms such as Bondora and Swaper can be more transparent in the future, since "everything comes from one source" on these platforms. The procurement of loans and their provision in the market come from the same companies. These processes become more difficult when loan-takers are involved as on Mintos. Here you have to work carefully during the selection process for new loan originators. Loan originators with an audit by KPMG or similar accountancy firms are definitely better in my favor. These also come in our auto-invest much faster than other loan lenders without such a test.

In general, security is probably the key to any investment. The risk at P2P is simply higher because of the young age. There was no real crisis in this industry. To better assess which areas are particularly risky, take a look at the following chart. Here, the top section identifies the risk of fraud in each industry branch. According to the surveyed platforms, the risk is particularly high in the trading of invoices, better known as factoring.

With a 33% rating as highly prone to fraud, P2P beginners are more likely to avoid this area. Also, platforms with a very high proportion of factoring loans should rather be avoided by beginners, since the disintegration of such a platform is due to a fraud and also in itself higher. As shown in the bottom section, 55% of the surveyed platforms estimate that the risk of bankruptcy for a factoring platform is high to very high. However, this value is very high for all four industry sectors concerned. This does not mean that money is misappropriated or misused in another context. P2P is simply a young industry in which bankruptcies are not unlikely.

Figure 27: Risk Factors by Debt-based Models

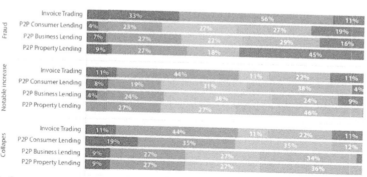

Risk factors

Most important, however, is the increase in risks, shown in the middle section. Here it becomes clear that, apart from factoring, other industry branches have been able to detect a much smaller, if any, increase in the risk. An increase in the risk of consumer credit is rated as low to very low at 44%, while 27% see a high to a very high increase in risk. So we have a reasonably well-balanced field. Consumer loans also seem to remain the perennial favorite in P2P, with 33.8% of the total market in 2016 being consumer credit. Investors can thus simply avoid riskier parts such as factoring and still encounter a large number of available loans.

30. ARE P2P LOANS SUSTAINABLE?

The question arising from the title of this chapter is anything but easy to answer, because the future is never predictable, and this is especially true of any type of investment. Even historical data, from which speculative inferences are possible, exists for the P2P asset class barely. So we can only speculate where the path will eventually go.

The fact is that P2P providers in all loan segments (for example private loans for companies, private financing of aircraft, etc.) and countries are rapidly developing, with more and more new ones. This trend is likely to continue for now at first, because there is currently nothing that speaks against it. But that does not mean that nothing can happen tomorrow that will limit the development of these markets completely (for example, legislative changes or a financial market crash).

At present, the trend among some providers is very strong, and their brokers are also opening their doors across the borders of the European or world market. Bondora, for example, has gradually expanded its negotiations to countries such as Spain and Slovakia, with Slovakia now being taken out of the assortment. Mintos, meanwhile, even operates worldwide in countries like Kenya and China.

For both borrowers and lenders, this opens up new opportunities, and it is well known it is now possible to invest money on many foreign P2P platforms (which has not always been this way). Other providers are currently doing the same, so in all likelihood, the opportunities for investing in personal loans and their ease of use will continue to increase, not only across Europe but also worldwide. Of course, this will not only bring benefits but also provide for opacity and confusion. Therefore, it is all the more important to build early-based knowledge of the P2P market, if you intend to invest there safely and with understanding in the long term.

Furthermore, as investors, we should know that the P2P market is still growing rapidly and that we have not used the potential of this asset class by far compared to, say, the US. For comparison, let's take a look at the approximate credit volumes of the largest providers from Germany, the United Kingdom and the United States:

Auxmoney.com (DE): about 100 million euros a year
Zopa (GB): about 1 billion pounds a year
LendingClub.com (US): about $ 6 billion a year [91]

Based on these figures, we can assume that existing and new providers will (have to) do a lot to increase their lending volume. For example, in Germany at the time of writing, there is hardly a P2P platform that offers a mobile app, which means that investors can also react quickly on the go. Furthermore, insurers could jump into the P2P market and hedge investors' capital, building up additional investor confidence.

The investment insurance concept for P2P loans already exists and was originally created in China, after some employees of the management of the P2P platform "Wangwangda" with parts of the managed funds of investors disappeared without a trace. Current pilot projects are in the US (Lemonade, Jointly and Ledger Investing[92]). And also in conversation with the Latvian platform DoFinance when we were in Riga in 2018, there were ideas to additionally secure loans. We are very excited about what the future development looks like in this topic.

Another very ingenious outlook on the potential of the P2P industry is provided by the book "The End of Banking" by Jonathan McMillan[93]. The issue here is how to prevent the state from stepping in for bank debt in times of crisis. The author is of the opinion that banks in today's system accept short-term deposits from customers, but resell them too long-term and expensive to customers. With this

---

[91] Online comparison from the portal boerse-online.de from March 2015

[92] See also https://en.wikipedia.org/wiki/Peer-to-peer_insurance

[93] Further information in the literature recommendations

philosophy, banks are legally granting more loans than their financial contributions cover. In order to keep this system operational and to secure the investors' investments, there is the deposit insurance (the amount and severity vary from country to country). But this also means that banks do not have to be cautious when lending, because they lose not their own money and can, as the recent financial crisis showed, trust that the state will jump in an emergency.

As a solution to this problem, the authors propose the open loan market (P2P lending) to only lend out loans, which were also certainly financed in advance - namely by the investors. A proposal that is unlikely to be fully implemented, but provides much food for thought and information on the possibilities of this industry. The first steps in this direction have already been taken; British P2P facilitator Funding Circle and Spanish Santander Bank have recently been working hand in hand to provide borrowers with cash[94]. Other banks are also thinking about cooperating with P2P platforms or even adding their own platform to the regular banking business (for example Commerzbank[95]).

So in conclusion, as we said in the introduction to this chapter, we cannot really predict the future of the P2P industry. There are still a lot of uncertainties, but also many opportunities for growth. We can say that suppliers have to do a lot to create transparency and trust. Each vendor must make it clear to potential investors what they are going to do in the "Investing in Personal Loans" adventure. Investors should, for example, know in advance what the credit default statistics look like, how the provider's return is calculated and much more. Some of these data are still difficult to deploy because many companies are quite young. An indicator of loan defaults for a provider that has only existed for a year or less is, logically, of little value.

---

[94] https://www.fundingcircle.com/blog/2014/06/funding-circle-santander-announce-partnership-support-thousands-uk-businesses/
[95] http://www.p2p-banking.com/countries/germany-commerzbank-will-launch-p2p-lending-platform-main-funders-next-week/

Industry growth requires interested borrowers and lenders, and these must be equally promoted and sponsored. Due to the mass of P2P providers, which are currently flowing into the market year after year, it is not clear at the present time which providers will ultimately survive. Therefore, the decision on a long-term investment should also be considered and decided with great care. Please note our checklist for supplier selection from the corresponding chapter.

31. INVESTMENT ETHICS

Very often, the argument used in P2P loans is that it is morally unreasonable to invest in this form of investment. And in almost every conversation about it, at some point, this topic comes up.

"I do not give anyone a loan that does not manage to handle money on their own. I would only make his life worse!"

This is how the arguments usually look like. Well, if we are part of this conversation, it usually goes something like this:

Us: "Well, what are you investing in?"
P2P-opponent: "Only passive with ETFs on the stock exchange. I participate in the world economy and that is much better business than P2P!"
Us: "I see, the MSCI World contains more than 1,600 companies from 23 countries. They all work so much better than you do when you give a car loan to Mr. Meier from Berlin?"
P2P-opponent: "Well, yes… hmmmm…."

You could also add other things here (such as ignorance of the management of instant access savings account), but that would unnecessarily expand the fictional conversation and ultimately always say the same thing. No investment is morally 100% acceptable to everyone. It always depends on your personal point of view and you always have to ask yourself: "Will I invest or do I want to improve the world with every breath?" Do not get us wrong: Investment should not mean that we cannot improve the world (because in the end, we will do just that). But first of all, investment does not have this purpose. You do not invest your money to save black swans from extinction, but to increase your wealth in the long run.

But why is there always this discussion on P2P loans? Well, let's take a look at the German Auxmoney provider as an example:

Sample loan Auxmoney

At Auxmoney, it's easy to see what a borrower actually wants the money from. In this case, namely for a compensation of his credit line. But if you bring your money to the bank and they pass it on, there is no moral discussion - because you cannot see what your money will be used for. The bank will know what it is doing. From the transparency advantage of P2P loans (which you can choose yourself) is, therefore, morally rather a disadvantage.

The determination of the creditworthiness of banks is by no means better or different than from the P2P platforms. They work with large, recognized and experienced credit bureaus such as the Schufa or Arvato Infoscore. It's just our habit that does not allow us to just give people that money, and we see exactly what the money is used for.

If we look at the Baltics on platforms like Mintos, we realize that the problem has already been detected there or they never intended to publish too much information about the borrower to the lenders.

Darlehensangaben

Darlehenstyp	Verbraucherkredit
Darlehensbetrag	€ 231
Ausstehende Restschuld	€ 231
Zinssatz	11.1%
LTV	-
Anfangslaufzeit	1 m.
Verbliebene Darlehenslaufzeit	29 d.
Abschreibungsmethode	Full
Listing Date	08.09.2016
Ausgabedatum	07.09.2016
Enddatum	07.10.2016
Status	Aktuell
Darlehensanbahner	Lendo

Aufgliederung der Investitionen

Lendo - 57% / € 131
8 Investorenanteile - 43% / € 100

Dieser Kredit kommt mit einer Rückkaufga
den Investoren zurückkaufen, wenn er 60

Kreditnehmer   Zahlungsplan   Aufgliederung der Investitionen

Angaben zum Kreditnehmer

Kreditnehmer	Weiblich, 49
Darlehenszweck	Verbraucherkredit
Staat	Georgia

Sample loan Mintos

The information about the borrower is very meager. You no longer see what he (or in this case, she) would like to take out the loan for and the pure investment moves more into the foreground. For us as passive investors a sensible measure. Because let's face it, who the hell cares what someone needs your money for? At the end of the day, he may have stated something that is not true anyway. The important thing is that he keeps his contract, uses the money and you get the promised repayment or return. It may well be that you make a slightly better return with manual loan selection, but this may as well be based on chance. Our first investments, for example, were also manual nature but not more really successful, although we have carefully selected the loans and paid attention only to the highest credit rating.

Another point is that the basic assumption that only private bankrupts would borrow money to pay their casino debts is not only discriminatory but simply wrong! We have already given people loans for their studies, their real estate financing or their business idea. The self-employed people in particular often have the problem that they are difficult to obtain loans from traditional commercial banks, even if their business is running well and they can deposit collateral.

I still remember very well the personal story of an Austrian friend of my wife. He is an independent English teacher and had not been granted credit for his house because of his self-employment. When I heard the conversation over Skype in the background and then mentioned the P2P platforms, this friend has informed himself and actually received his online loan. Now he already lives in the new house.

Of course, you can still invest manually if you feel better about it. Ultimately, that's one of the big advantages of P2P. Due to the often given transparency and the possibility to invest both passively and actively, the choice of the loan is in the end completely up to you.

You do not want to give anyone a loan so he can balance his money with your money? No problem, just do not do it and support someone who, for example, uses your money to start his own business. We believe that you should decide whether you want to invest or put a high value on the ethical component. Responsibility about finances rests with everyone. Certainly, some of us are better or worse off than others, but everyone has the opportunity to build and apply fundamental knowledge about how to handle finances.

Because of the information provided to us, we do not want to make a decision about who gets our money and who does not. It would be like sorting out written applications and making assumptions without getting to know the candidate himself (which, unfortunately, is normal). As you can see from this discussion, the transparency of an investment product not only has good sides but quite a lot of pitfalls as well. The secret here is rather to find the golden mean between too much and too little information.

32. SUMMARY

written by Daniel Korth, the financial rocker
finanzrocker.net

My learnings from the P2P investments

The P2P loan market is growing more and more, and as you learned in this book, there are many good ways to invest. Even if the risk of default is due to the high return, there is nothing wrong with spreading his money. However, the overall portfolio share of P2P loans should not outgrow - more likely in the single-digit or low double-digit range.

When I started investing in German P2P loans a few years ago, it was still an adventure. At that time, there were only a few platforms and nobody knew where the path would lead. Since then, the volume on the German P2P marketplaces alone has more than doubled. The music plays primarily in the Baltic States. Mintos, Bondora, Viainvest or Estateguru are growing enormously and are enjoying increasing popularity.

But my way actually led me through the two German platforms Lendico and Auxmoney, which could not be more different. While Lendico has caused three-digit losses and now hardly offers any loans, Auxmoney is expanding enormously. Nevertheless, the largest German P2P platform has not developed so well for me. Some defaults and a return of only 6% are too little given the risk involved. Especially with minimum investment sums of 25 euros, the diversification is much too short.

With only 100 euros spent, I can invest in ten loans on many of the Baltic platforms and spread across multiple countries. That does not work with the German platforms. Incidentally, this also applies to real estate crowdfunding, where a minimum stake of 500 euros is often a requirement. For a conservative investor like me, that's a clear disadvantage. In addition, the close connection to an additional German account turned out to be an absolute disadvantage.

While Lendico has canceled the partnership with Wirecard Bank and I now receive mini-contributions every week, at the Fintech Group Bank which is connected to Auxmoney, you have to pay a penalty on the account balance. Although the P2P provider will take over for the first, it raises the question of how long that will be the case.

Regulations or not, everything works better with the Baltic platforms. I get clear bank statements, see at a glance, where it hooks and a transfer does not take 24 hours. That's how I invest faster and am also very broad-based. This is the absolute prerequisite for both equity investments and P2P platforms to reduce the risk of loss. That's why every P2P investor should always spread across multiple platforms, not just investing in big names like Bondora or Mintos.

In this book by Lars Wrobbel and Kolja Barghoorn, you've gotten to know all the major platforms and, based on the detailed descriptions, you can decide for yourself where to take the first (or second) steps. Back then, the book helped me decide on more P2P platforms and try out different ones.

Meanwhile, I do not want to worry about my P2P investments anymore. Everything should run automatically and the repaid money should be automatically reinvested again. Thanks to the buyback guarantees, the defaults on the Baltic platforms in my portfolio are very limited, but these guarantees may only be on paper in the event of a real crisis. But as long as they are not there, I continue to invest in my pre-determined limits.

Per platform, this limit is 1,000 euros for me. Maybe you'll say, "Oh, that's not so much". But in view of the increased risk, it is for me personally the border that I wouldn't like to cross. Nevertheless, the platforms generate me a few hundred euros a year and grow by the compound interest effect on and on.

The yields can be monitored particularly well via the "Portfolio Performance" open-source software. For this, I have created my own P2P account, where I enter all interest, withdrawals and losses once a month. Of course, you can also do this on each platform, but I personally missed the overview. It was too much for me to keep six accounts for a few percent of my portfolio. On average, I get a return on the Baltic platforms of 11.3% per annum, while German underperformer platforms are below 5%. With a few simple steps, I get a decent return and in contrast to my numerous equity investments, I do not have to do anything.

The interest on the loans I see as an additional dividend, which increases each year. At the moment, I only invest regularly new money on one platform and that's Estateguru. Personally, I have a very good feeling here, because the platform offers P2P loans for real estate projects and secures them with the land or the real estate. Mintos itself, I see increasingly critical, because of the extremely strong growth on loan lenders, currencies and countries. This creates new risks for the investor, which cannot always be fully understood. The bankruptcy of the lender Eurocent was the best example.

Even though I have focused on securities as a stock investor, I am very pleased with my P2P experience over the past three years. How the platforms evolve remains to be seen. In general, there are now too many platforms that also serve the same markets. New features such as "Go & Grow" by Bondora ensure that the platforms differ from each other and evolve.

However, the investor should not underestimate the risks for all returns and interesting functions. In the next crisis, it will become clear to what extent the loans can be repaid. That's why you should diversify widely into P2P loans and invest on sight. So you will have a good feeling in the end.

33. CLOSING WORDS

Now that you've read and learned a lot about P2P, the platforms, the techniques, etc., we'd like to share our final opinion. There are certainly many uncertainties, disadvantages and a lot of work ahead of you if you want to be successful in this asset class in the long term. However, investing in the P2P asset class is, in our view, an interesting alternative to your existing portfolio due to its very low correlation to the stock market. Furthermore, it fits the basic principles of an intelligent investor. Leaning on this, Gerald Hörhan once said, "It's better to own debt than to have it." He's absolutely right, and by investing in the P2P market, we have this opportunity in the simplest possible way right now.

We also like the current selection of providers and the low costs very well. There is pretty much something for every taste. Every provider has its advantages and features here and there, but the development is far from over. We are very curious to see what the future will be like and which providers will prevail at the end with which features. We also hope that other interesting providers outside of Germany or even Europe will be added.

Our trip to the Baltics 2018 has once again shown that it is really happening behind the scenes and that the platforms are bringing one innovation after another onto the market. For example, the Latvian platform Viainvest told us about the idea of linking the P2P lending market to the crypto market. In the meantime, it is no longer an idea, but a product that is already accessible to some European citizens.[96]

It will also be interesting to see how the investor community will develop. Despite the fourth edition in 2018, our book is one of the few that deals with specific P2P platforms, investor strategies, and related P2P execution tools, and we hope that many more will follow from other authors. The material and the possibilities are available in any case and also the community[97] is growing day by day. So there

---

[96] More information at https://www.cryptoloan.se/en
[97] We would be pleased to welcome you here as well in:

is much to discover, develop and research with the intention of ultimately improving our return on investment.

So, now it's up to you to internalize the tips from our book and, on that basis, develop your personal strategy to finally reap the rewards of your efforts with a good return. Of course, if the P2P market is not for you, then that's perfectly fine too, because the book has its use and purpose for this decision as well. No matter what you do, always remember: do not react headlong and immediately start charging! Let an idea mature first. Even important decisions should lie for a while. Because it's all about getting things done right, and it's always better to reach the goal slowly than not to reach it.

Finally, we would like to thank our guest authors once again: they rounded off the book and added value with their extensive expert knowledge. Your web pages are a great resource for every P2P investor.

A small request to conclude to you: In this book, the blog, the videos and the ever-growing Facebook community put a lot of work and our personal time. We would, therefore, be delighted to receive **honest** feedback from you, as this is a validation of our hard, disciplined and persevering work and enables us to expand, improve or even provide additional help for you. If you want to support us, please leave us a review on Amazon.com.

Reviews are an extremely important part of products. Customers rely on your review when faced with the decision to buy this book as well. Certain reviews have probably also been the reason why you are reading this book. Your review will help our books become more visible on Amazon. So if you liked the book, we would be grateful for a review. To leave a rating, log in to your account and go to the "Invest in P2P Lending" product page, scroll to the bottom and click "Write Review".

---

https://www.facebook.com/groups/p2pcommunity/ - our P2P community there is a free and lively exchange on various investor issues.

> Sagen Sie Ihre Meinung zu diesem Artikel
>
> Kundenrezension verfassen >

Alternatively, you can go to My Account> My Orders and post a review there after clicking on the book title.

We like to read every review and also every personal feedback to us. This helps us to improve our book for you bit by bit. We esteem your appreciation of this book. A book lives, and it lives through you!

You can also contact us by e-mail if you want. We are always looking forward to receiving personal messages, and suggestions for improvement or ideas for other topics that could help other P2P investors improve their investment. So please do not hesitate to write to us; every single email is read, all the ideas are collected and rated, and then you may soon find exactly your topic or proposed idea in the next edition, on the P2P blog or in the community discussion board.

Contact:
Kolja: kolja@aktienmitkopf.de
Lars: lars@passives-einkommen-mit-p2p.de

In this spirit, we sincerely thank you for the trust you have placed in us with the purchase of this book and hope very much that it could live up to your expectations. We wish you every success in all asset classes in which you are on the go!

Kolja Barghoorn & Lars Wrobbel

34. ABOUT KOLJA & LARS

Kolja Barghoorn and Lars Wrobbel have been business partners in P2P investments and book publishing since 2014. Over the years, they have created a lot of content and activities. There are many YouTube videos, podcasts, books and interviews among them. They can usually be found together at the INVEST financial fair in Stuttgart, which they have been accompanying together since 2015.

Kolja and Lars 2018 at Mintos in Riga

The two are currently planning a fixed community meeting on the subject of P2P loans in the Baltic States, where they want to use the local platforms to familiarise investors with the various business models.[98]

---

[98] https://p2pconference.com/

---

35. THE P2P-INVESTOR-TELEGRAM

Although investing in P2P loans may seem very simple, you should know exactly how it all works and how best to use this asset class in your portfolio. To help you understand how P2P loans work and the basics of passive income, we invite you to subscribe to the P2P Investor Telegram.

The P2P Investor Telegram is completely free, and after you sign up, Lars will send you all the information you need about your P2P investment on a regular basis. You'll learn new things every 2 weeks in short, concise emails.

The 14-day P2P Investor Telegram brings you a lot more interesting content. At irregular intervals, you will be given access to exclusive promotions that are only sent to subscribers.

The highlights in detail:

- Direct information and link to the latest article about the publication in your e-mail inbox
- Current news from the P2P sector of the respective calendar weeks
- News about the blog of Lars and upcoming events
- Exclusive bonus promotions only for recipients of the investor telegram
- The current top topics from the community

You can log in under:
https://passives-einkommen-mit-p2p.de/p2p-investoren-telegramm/

36. LITERATURE RECOMMENDATIONS

Finally, we would like to give you a few suggestions for further book purchases, which we consider to be useful, either because we have read them ourselves and consider them valuable for any investment or because they have to do with the P2P asset class. Please note that these are mostly German titles. Check in individual cases whether there are also English versions available.

- P2P-Kredite – Marktplätze für Privatkredite im Internet von Fabian Blaesi (ISBN 3839149320)
- Peer-to-Peer Lending 101: Build Wealth and Create Passive Income Using Peer-to-Peer Lending von Marco Schwartz (ISBN 1533386390)
- Die Bank sind wir: Chancen und Perspektiven von Social Banking von Lothar Lochmaier (ISBN 393693164X)
- The LendingClub.com Story: How the world's largest peer to peer lender is transforming finance and how you can benefit von Peter Renton (ISBN 1481131737)
- Investment Punk: Warum ihr schuftet und wir reich werden von Gerald Hörhan (ISBN 3548373844)
- Intelligent Investieren: Der Bestseller über die richtige Anlagstrategie von Benjamin Graham (ISBN 3898798275)
- Souverän investieren mit Indexfonds und ETFs: Wie Privatanleger das Spiel gegen die Finanzbranche gewinnen von Gerd Kommer (ISBN 3593504545)
- Die Kunst, über Geld nachzudenken von André Kostolany (ISBN 3548375901)
- Money: Die 7 einfachen Schritte zur finanziellen Freiheit von Tony Robbins (ISBN 389879914X)
- Reich werden und bleiben: Ihr Wegweiser zur finanziellen Freiheit von Rainer Zitelmann (ISBN 3898799204)
- Cashflow Quadrant: Rich dad poor dad von Robert Kiyosaki (ISBN 3898795918)
- Der Schwarze Schwan: Die Macht höchst unwahrscheinlicher Ereignisse von Nassim Nicholas Taleb (ISBN 3423345969)

37. FURTHER SOURCES OF INFORMATION ON THE INTERNET

As always, valuable information can also be found on the Internet. Whether blogs, forums or the information provided by the P2P platforms themselves. In our opinion, the most valuable sources of information are listed below. Please also note here that they are mostly in the German language.

- passives-einkommen-mit-p2p.de – The blog of Lars. Launched at the end of 2015 and actually the most successful P2P blog in Germany with almost 100,000 interested readers every month. In addition to the book, it tries to keep you up to date and show you how to turn your P2P portfolio into a passive income. Some topics from the book can be found there, in a different or expanded form.
- p2p-anlage.de – On this page, Andreas Tielmann shows you well-researched information on current P2P topics. His monthly P2P provider rankings, which he creates himself, are particularly valuable in our eyes. He is also an expert on everything to do with the secondary market, which is why he kindly contributed a chapter to our book.
- p2p4oktaeder.blogspot.de – The p2p4oktaeder blog is a private investor blog. It reports in detail about experiences on various P2P platforms. We like to read his articles again and again.
- p2phero.com – The P2P Hero has been around for a long time, writes very in-depth articles and knows all about the subject matter. A must for every P2P investor.
- finanzrocker.net – Daniel Korth is almost a blogging legend when it comes to finances. As a "financial rocker" he always captivates with great new topics, including passive income, P2P and many other exciting FinTech articles. Make sure you check him out.
- p2p-kredite.com – Another valuable source is the website of Claus Lehmann, who reports regularly and competently on new topics in the P2P world. There is also an attached forum whose value as a source of information is enormous. Its site is probably

the best-known source of P2P information in Germany at the moment.

- lendacademy.com – The Lend Academy is an American blog by Peter Renton. Away from the European P2P market, you will find interesting information from the other side of the pond.
- lendingmemo.com – On LendingMemo Simon Cunningham writes about many interesting P2P topics and there are also free P2P education videos available. However, his blog has not been maintained since mid-2015.
- moneyisyourfriend.eu – Estonian teacher Kristi writes on her personal blog about the P2P investment and her financial goals.

This book is dedicated to myself, since a rational capitalist always first thinks of himself.

Therefore, all income is invested in equities in a self-serving and well-considered manner. But don't worry, in exchange for your money you will receive a lot of content that will make you rich and free in the long run. But realize that the path to becoming a capitalist is a hard piece of work that requires a willingness to learn, self-discipline and the courage to take risks. There are all too many dream dancers in this world who believe that you can easily become a millionaire on the stock exchange as a beginner, with 200 euros and a few shares in 5 years.

But only the rational capitalist will be successful in the long run!

Available as:
- eBook (ASIN B0785F2K27) 9.99 EUR
- Softcover (ISBN 1981127917) 23.99 EUR
- Hardcover (ISBN 3745062779) 38.99 EUR
- Audiobook (ASIN B079ZBH4P1) 25.95 EUR

39. LEGAL AND IMPRINT

Published by:
Barghoorn Finance S.L.
Calle Punta Ballena 18
Le Dauphin 12 B
ES - 07181 Torrenova - Mallorca
Spain

and

Lars Wrobbel
c/o
Papyrus Autoren-Club,
R.O.M. Logicware GmbH
Pettenkoferstr. 16-18
10247 Berlin
German

Printed in Great Britain
by Amazon

30061161R00098